Preparation *for* Citizenship

STECK-VAUGHN
ELEMENTARY · SECONDARY · ADULT · LIBRARY

A Harcourt Company

www.steck-vaughn.com

Acknowledgments

Staff Credits

Executive Editor: Ellen Northcutt
Associate Director of Design: Cynthia Ellis
Designer: Alexandra Corona
Electronic Production Artist: Linda Reed
Photo Researcher: Claudette Landry
Production Coordinator: Paula Schumann
Production Manager: Mychael Ferris

Photography Credits

Photo of George Washington on pp.iii, 2, 32, and 58: Gilbert Stuart, George Washington, Gift of Thomas Jefferson Coolidge IV in memory of his great-grandfather, Thomas Jefferson Coolidge, his grandfather, Thomas Jefferson Coolidge II, and his father, Thomas Jefferson Coolidge III, Photograph ©2001 Board of Trustees, National Gallery of Art, Washington.

Cover (people) ©Bob Daemmrich Photography, Inc.; (US flag) ©Corbis; (passport, passport photos, pencil) ©PhotoDisc; title page ©Corbis; p.iii (US capitol, fireworks) ©Corbis; p.iv ©PhotoDisc; pp.2b, 2c ©Corbis; p.4 National Archives, Still Picture Branch; p.5a "Clements Library, University of Michigan" King George III, W. Woollett (engraver), after A. Ramsey (painter) ca. 1760-1785; p.5b Courtesy of the Library of Congress; p.6a National Archives, Still Picture Branch; p.6b Independence Historical Park; pp.7a, 7b, 7c, 8a Courtesy of the Library of Congress; p.8b ©Corbis; p.9 Courtesy of the Library of Congress; pp.10a, 10b ©Corbis; p.12 Courtesy of the Library of Congress; p.13 Reagan Bradshaw/SV; p.14a National Archives and Records Administration; p.14b National Archives, Still Picture Branch; p.14c ©PhotoDisc; p.14d ©John Neubauer/PhotoEdit; p.15a ©AP/ Wide World Photos; p.15b ©Mary Kate Denny/PhotoEdit; p.15c ©Superstock; p.15d U.S. Immigration and Naturalization Service; pp.18a, 18b, 18c, 19a, 19b ©CORBIS; p.21 ©Bettmann/CORBIS; pp.22a, 22b Courtesy of the Franklin D. Roosevelt Library Digital Archives; p.23a UN Photo; p.23b ©AP/Wide World Photos; p.26a Photo No. W4/Spiegal in the John F. Kennedy Library; p.26b LBJ Library Photo by Cecil Stoughton; p.26c ©Wally McNamee/CORBIS; p.26d ©Bettmann/CORBIS; p.27 National Archives, Still Pictures Branch; pp.32b, 32c ©Corbis; p.34 ©Sipa Press; p.35a ©Bettmann/CORBIS; p.35b ©Paul Conklin/PhotoEdit; p.35c ©Bettmann/CORBIS; pp.35d, 36 ©Corbis; p.38 ©AP/Wide World Photo/White House/Eric Draper; p.39a ©AP/Wide World Photo/Eric Draper; p.39b ©Corbis; p.39c LBJ Library Photo by Cecil Stoughton; p.39d LBJ Library Photo by Cecil Stoughton; p.40 National Archives, Still Picture Branch; p.41 Courtesy of the Office of the President of the United States; p.42 ©AP/Wide World Photo/Roberto Borea; p.43a Supreme Court Historical Society; p.43b ©Corbis Sygma; pp.44, 46, 47a ©Corbis; p.47b ©Photodisc; p.50 ©AP Photo/Rogelio Solis; pp.51a, 51b ©AP/Wide World Photo/Ron Edmonds; pp.58b, 58c ©Corbis; p.60 ©Ken Fisher/Stone; p.61a Courtesy of the Pilgrim Society, Plymouth, Massachusetts; p.61b Lambert/Archive Photos; p.62 Courtesy of the Library of Congress; p.63 ©Ariel Skelley/The Stock Market; p.64 ©Corbis; p.65a Courtesy of the Library of Congress; p.65b Courtesy the Maryland Historical Society; p.65c The National Museum of American History, Smithsonian Museum; p.65d ©PhotoDisc; p.66 ©Corbis; p.68 ©Ariel Skelley/The Stock Market; p.69a Courtesy of the Library of Congress; p.69b National Archives, Still Pictures Branch; p.69c ©Robert Brenner/PhotoEdit; p.69d ©William A. Bake/CORBIS; p.69e ©James P. Blair/CORBIS; p.70a ©AP/Wide World Photos; p.70b ©Bob Fitch/Black Star; p.76 National Archives and Records Administration; p.77 The National Museum of American History, Smithsonian Museum.

ISBN 0-7398-3458-4

Contents

To the Learner

Congratulations! You are on your way to becoming a U.S. citizen. *Preparation for Citizenship* will help you get ready for the INS naturalization test and interview. When you finish this book, you will be able to answer many questions about the history of the United States. You will understand how the U.S. government works. In addition, you will learn other important facts about life in the United States.

At your INS interview, you need to show that you know English. As you study the lessons, you will get practice speaking, reading, and writing English. You will also have a chance to practice listening to and speaking with your classmates and your teacher.

We hope you enjoy learning about your new country. Good luck!

To the Instructor

Preparation for Citizenship is designed for non-native speakers of English who are also applicants for naturalization and want to prepare for the civics and English test and interview required by the Immigration and Naturalization Service (INS). *Preparation for Citizenship* features simple English and a variety of visual aids that highlight and clarify important facts and concepts. The program is suitable for English as a Second Language learners at beginning through low-intermediate levels.

The instructional material in *Preparation for Citizenship* is based on the questions and answers on U.S. history and government provided by the INS. Each lesson focuses on a key topic, and the instructional sequence is designed to help learners master new vocabulary and sentence patterns at the same time that they are learning new information. The accompanying CD focuses on the information learners will need in order to succeed during the INS test and interview.

To the Learner

The first time you present the program to learners, you may wish to read the *To the Learner* section with the class. Point out that English language skills are an important part of the INS test and interview process and explain that the *Preparation for Citizenship* book and CD will give them confidence with this process.

Unit Overview

Preparation for Citizenship is divided into three units: U.S. history, U.S. government, and U.S. celebrations.

Unit Opener   Each unit opener features a photograph, a timeline, and several discussion questions. These elements place the material in context, identify the key content to be covered, and encourage learners to share what they already know about the topic.

The Unit Opener provides a framework for the study of several individual lessons. Begin by having learners look at the featured photo and asking them to tell you what they see. Read the questions aloud and encourage learners to answer as well as they can. This allows them to recognize what they know and builds confidence in their ability to master the material. Invite learners to explain what they think they will learn and encourage them to make up questions of their own. The timeline draws students into the content of the unit. Briefly discuss each item on the timeline, paraphrasing and explaining in simple English as needed. Invite learners to name similar events from the history of their countries.

Checkup Each unit concludes with a *Checkup* that lets you and your learners assess how well they have mastered the material in the unit. These pages provide test-taking practice with multiple-choice questions. *Talk About It,* at the end of the *Checkup,* is an opportunity for self-assessment and individual goal-setting.

How to Teach a Lesson

All lessons follow a similar format, including a preview of what students will learn and a vocabulary list, *Words to Know.* This is followed by pages of activities designed to help learners make use of all four language skills to master the content. Each lesson ends with a *Figure It Out* activity. These pages provide a final review as well as an informal assessment of how well learners have mastered the material.

The following is a list of suggestions for how to make use of each segment of a lesson. But before you read further, remember that the key to your learners' success is to get them involved. Adults bring a wealth of information and experience to the learning process. Helping them activate this background information will have a positive effect on their ability to make sense of what they read and hear in class. Comparing and contrasting the history, government, and celebrations of the United States with those of their native countries will open communication and increase their rate of success.

Lesson Opener

Preview Read the list aloud and invite learners to share what they already know about each item. You can also have learners discuss the list in small groups before they present their ideas to the class.

Words to Know The words on this list are presented in the order in which they appear in the lesson. In most cases, only the base form of the word appears. Read each word aloud and have learners pronounce it several times. Then invite learners to explain the meanings of the words they already know by using each one in a sentence. Define any unfamiliar terms in simple English. Use pictures or sample sentences to clarify the meaning. Use a bilingual dictionary if appropriate.

Pictures and Captions Every lesson includes multiple photographs and paintings with captions that describe the picture. As you begin each lesson, have learners preview the pictures and speculate about what they are going to learn. Later, as learners work with individual pages, point out the pictures again. Read the captions together and discuss how the pictures relate to what they are learning.

Read About It   Have learners read each section silently before you read it aloud, play the CD, or have a student read it to the class. Then talk about it with the class. Learners may want to ask questions or discuss vocabulary words from the reading. Then ask some simple factual questions to review the content. Most pages have an additional teaching suggestion at the bottom—*See for Yourself, Partner Work, Group Work,* or *Class Discussion.* All of them encourage learners to learn from each other, extend their productive use of English, reinforce concepts and vocabulary, and prepare for the INS interview.

See for Yourself   Have pairs of learners identify or place various geographical locations on the U.S. and world maps on pages 76 and 77. Encourage them to share their work with other pairs or with the whole class.

Partner Work   Have pairs of learners review the page. By reading aloud and writing dictated sentences, they prepare for the dictation or reading section of the citizenship test.

Group Work   Have learners do this activity in groups of three or four. You may wish to appoint a leader for each group. This person keeps his or her book open and provides language support to the other learners as needed.

Class Discussion   Have learners write their questions before they present them to the class. Encourage several learners to respond to each question, giving additional information as appropriate.

Write It Down   The activities on these pages present and review content and provide writing practice. Ask learners to take turns reading this material aloud to their partners as preparation for the dictation or reading part of the citizenship test.

Talk It Over   *Talk It Over* sections introduce and reinforce the vocabulary and concepts in each lesson. Since these dialogs are good opportunities for learners to develop their listening and speaking skills, they also provide valuable preparation for the INS interview. Read the dialogs aloud or have learners listen to the CD.

Figure It Out   Learners fill in missing words in sentences, complete crossword puzzles, note correct answers on a chart, etc. These exercises are a final review of the lesson and give practice with speaking, reading, and writing. Initially, you may need to model these activities on the board; however, as soon as possible, have learners take charge, doing the exercise in groups, in pairs, or individually.

Additional Materials

About the Bill of Rights (page 74)   This is a simple explanation of the Bill of Rights. After discussing its content with learners, you may wish to have pairs of learners cut the page into ten sections. Suggest that they write the number of the amendment on the back of each section, shuffle the slips of paper, and place them face down on the desk. Then have them choose a slip, read the number to a partner, and have that person describe the right or rights associated with that amendment.

The Star-Spangled Banner (page 75)   Many learners will need help understanding the words to the national anthem. Make a copy for each learner and discuss the meaning of each line. Bring a recording to class for a sing-along or cloze activity. Have learners bring in a recording or sing their country's national anthem.

United States and World Maps (pages 76 and 77)   Use these maps to provide geographical orientation when discussing key events in the United States and around the world. For example, in Lesson 3 have learners find the Confederate states, and in Lesson 4, have them say where they would put the Allied powers.

Application for Naturalization (Form N-400) (pages 78 – 84)   Learners can use this form to review the required information they will have to provide to the INS as part of the naturalization process. Learners may copy this form and fill it out for practice; however, they should know that the pages have been reduced in size. NOTE: *Do not assume the role of legal advisor to your learners.* Consult with local organizations that offer free or low-cost legal assistance and suggest that learners seek help there.

Citizenship Questions and Answers (pages 85 – 89)   These questions and answers have been provided by the INS. However, the order of the questions on this list has been changed so that it is grouped by topic and matches the order in which the information is presented in this book. Encourage learners to use these questions to test themselves over and over so that they feel completely comfortable at their INS interview. Model for them how to fold the pages down the middle so that they see only the question. If possible, role-play an INS interview with each learner. These mock interviews reinforce content, provide important practice with language skills, and help bolster learners' confidence. Whenever possible, have students listen to the questions on the CD so that they are exposed to a variety of voices.

Sentences for Dictation and Reading (pages 90 – 91)   This is a list of sample sentences for English testing, also provided by the INS. They are examples of the types of sentences an INS officer may ask applicants to read or write during their interview. Since the dictated sentences part of the citizenship process can be frightening to many learners, you can help by familiarizing them with the process. Dictate or play from the CD two or three sentences during each class period.

Questions and Answers for the 65/20 Exception (page 92)   These questions are for applicants who are at least 65 years old and have been living in the United States for at least 20 years. Applicants must answer six of ten questions correctly to pass. They may be tested in the language of their choice. Again, ensure that learners listen to the questions on the CD to give them experience listening to voices other than yours.

The Oath of Allegiance (page 93)   Before applicants can become citizens, they attend a ceremony and take the Oath of Allegiance to the United States. To help prepare your learners for what they will have to say at their ceremony, play the CD. Stop and pause at different breaks to allow learners to repeat the oath.

Answer Key (pages 94–96)   The Answer Key contains the answers to all the exercises in the book. Encourage learners to complete each exercise before consulting the answer key.

CD

The *Preparation for Citizenship* CD contains all of the information presented on the lesson openers, the *Read About It* and *Talk It Over* pages, the *Citizenship Questions and Answers*, the *Sentences for Dictation and Reading*, and the *Questions and Answers for the 65/20 Exception*. Using the CD helps learners prepare for the citizenship test and interview by exposing them to a variety of native speakers, so encourage learners to use the CD whenever possible. All listening activities are marked with this CD logo.

Helpful Web Sites

- Immigration and Naturalization Service
  http://www.ins.usdoj.gov
- National Center for ESL Literacy
  www.cal.org/ncle
- The National Immigration Forum
  http://www.immigrationforum.org/index.htm
- American Civil Liberties Union
  http://www.aclu.org/issues/immigrant/hmir.html

1

Unit 1

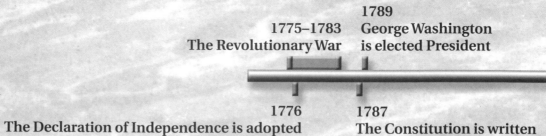

1775–1783
The Revolutionary War

1789
George Washington
is elected President

1776
The Declaration of Independence is adopted

1787
The Constitution is written

2

U.S. History

What do you know about the history of the United States?

★ **What was the Revolutionary War?**

★ **Who was George Washington?**

★ **What is the Constitution?**

★ **What was the Civil War?**

1941
The United
States enters
World War II

1914–1918
World War I

1861–1865
The Civil War

1939–1945
World War II

Lesson 1

The Revolutionary War

After you finish this lesson, you will be able to talk about

* ★ the Revolutionary War
* ★ Thomas Jefferson
* ★ the Declaration of Independence
* ★ George Washington
* ★ the Cabinet

 ## Words to Know

Practice saying these words.

★ colony	★ President	★ liberty
★ law	★ create	★ pursuit
★ fight	★ advise	★ death
★ independent	★ write	★ adopt
★ government	★ equal	★ leader
★ Commander in Chief	★ life	★ announce

The colonists started a war against England.

 The United States began as thirteen colonies ruled by England. The colonists were unhappy. They started the Revolutionary War in 1775 to fight for their independence.

4

Look and read.

King George III

King George III was king of England and the American colonies. The colonists didn't like his laws.

The Revolutionary War

The colonists fought to have their own government and to be independent from England.

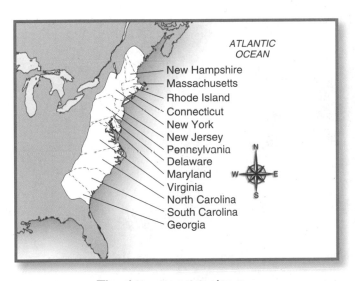

ATLANTIC OCEAN

New Hampshire
Massachusetts
Rhode Island
Connecticut
New York
New Jersey
Pennsylvania
Delaware
Maryland
Virginia
North Carolina
South Carolina
Georgia

The thirteen original states

The thirteen colonies became the thirteen original states. They were Virginia, Massachusetts, Maryland, Rhode Island, Connecticut, New Hampshire, North Carolina, South Carolina, New York, New Jersey, Pennsylvania, Delaware, and Georgia.

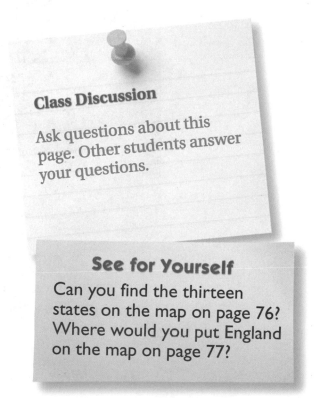

Class Discussion

Ask questions about this page. Other students answer your questions.

See for Yourself

Can you find the thirteen states on the map on page 76? Where would you put England on the map on page 77?

Look and read.

George Washington

George Washington was the first Commander in Chief of the U.S. Army and Navy. Later he became the first President of the United States. Americans call George Washington the "Father of our Country."

George Washington and his Cabinet

President Washington wanted help making decisions for the new country. He created the Cabinet. The Cabinet is the special group that advises the President.

Group Work

Work in groups. Close the book and say the main ideas on this page in your own words.

Read About It

Look and read.

Thomas Jefferson

Thomas Jefferson was the main writer of the Declaration of Independence.

Writing the Declaration of Independence

The Declaration of Independence said that all men are created equal and have the right to life, liberty, and the pursuit of happiness.

Patrick Henry

Patrick Henry was an American colonist. He said, "Give me liberty or give me death."

Partner Work

Take turns. Read the sentences to your partner. Your partner writes the sentences.

7

Look and read.

Signing the Declaration of Independence

The Declaration of Independence was adopted on July 4, 1776. Leaders from the thirteen colonies signed the Declaration of Independence. It said that the colonies were independent from England.

The first U.S. flag

When the Revolutionary War ended, the thirteen colonies were called states. Americans called their new country the United States of America. The new flag had thirteen stars and thirteen stripes, one star and one stripe for each state.

Group Work

Work in groups. Close the book and say the main ideas on this page in your own words.

8

Write the sentences.

1. George Washington was our first President. He created the Cabinet system.

   _____

   _____

2. Thomas Jefferson and other leaders wrote the Declaration of Independence.

   _____

   _____

3. The Declaration of Independence said that all men are created equal.

   _____

   _____

4. The Declaration of Independence also said that all men have the right to life, liberty, and the pursuit of happiness.

   _____

   _____

Partner Work

Take turns. Read the sentences to your partner. Your partner writes the sentences.

George Washington

Read About It

Look and read.

Independence Hall

American leaders met at Independence Hall in Philadelphia, Pennsylvania, to sign the Declaration of Independence. The Declaration of Independence was adopted on July 4, 1776.

The Liberty Bell

On that day, the Liberty Bell rang at Independence Hall. The Liberty Bell rang to announce America's independence from England.

See for Yourself

Can you find Pennsylvania on the map on page 76?

Group Work

Work in groups. Close the book and say the main ideas on this page in your own words.

10

Figure It Out

Complete the dialogs. Use the words from the boxes.

> George Washington Father Revolutionary War
> colonies President

A: In the _____, Americans fought against England.

B: That's right. At that time there were thirteen American _____.

A: _____ was the first Commander in Chief of the U.S. Army and Navy.

B: He was also our first _____.

A: That's why we call him the "_____ of our Country."

> England Thomas Jefferson Independence
> equal Declaration

A: What was the Declaration of _____?

B: It said the colonies were independent from _____.

A: Who was the main writer of the _____ of Independence?

B: _____. He wrote that all men are created _____.

Practice the dialogs with a partner.

The Constitution

After you finish this lesson, you will be able to talk about

★ the Constitution
★ the Preamble
★ the Bill of Rights

Words to Know

Practice saying these words.

★ supreme
★ amendment
★ change
★ rights
★ guarantee
★ speech

★ free
★ peaceable assembly
★ peacefully
★ petition
★ citizen
★ vote

★ benefit
★ apply for
★ federal
★ passport
★ relative

Signing the
Constitution

Leaders from the new states wrote the Constitution in 1787.
The Constitution is the supreme law of the land. There are
27 amendments, or changes, to the Constitution. They
guarantee the rights of all people living in the United States.

Talk It Over

Practice the dialog with a partner.

A: What's the Preamble?

B: The Preamble is the first part of the Constitution. It begins, "We the people of the United States . . . ."

A: What's an amendment?

B: An amendment is a change to the Constitution.

A: How many amendments are there?

B: There are 27, including the Bill of Rights.

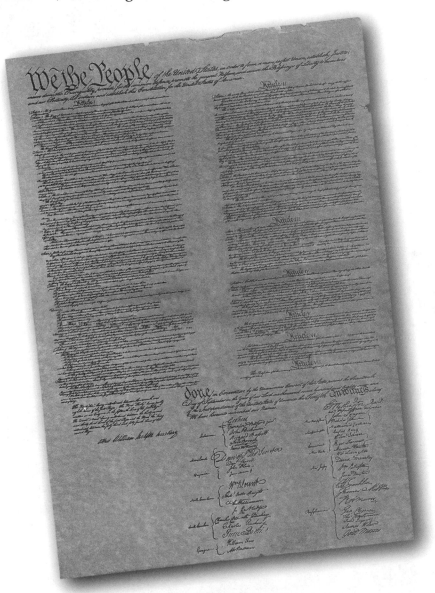

The Constitution

Look and read.

The Bill of Rights

The Bill of Rights is the first ten amendments to the Constitution. The Constitution and the Bill of Rights guarantee the rights of all people living in the United States. The government cannot take these rights away.

Freedom of speech

The First Amendment guarantees freedom of speech. People are free to say what they believe.

Peaceable assembly

Congress cannot take away the right to peaceable assembly. People are free to meet peacefully in groups.

Signing a petition

The Bill of Rights guarantees the right to petition, or ask, the government to change.

See for Yourself

If you are interested in reading more about the Bill of Rights, turn to page 74.

Read About It

🔘 **Look and read.**

Voting

The most important right of citizens is the right to vote. A citizen must be 18 years old to vote. The 15th, 19th, and 26th amendments guarantee voting rights.

This man has a government job working for the post office.

U.S. citizens have many benefits. For example, they can apply for federal government jobs. They can also travel with a U.S. passport.

Keeping the family together

U.S. citizens can bring close relatives to the United States.

Form N-400

Form N-400, Application for Naturalization, is used to apply for naturalized citizenship.

Partner Work

Take turns. Read the sentences to your partner. Your partner writes the sentences.

15

Complete the puzzle. Use the words from the box.

speech   Constitution   vote

amendment   Preamble   Rights

citizen

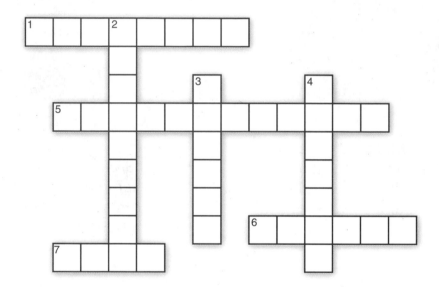

Across

1. The beginning of the Constitution is called the _____ .

5. The _____ is the supreme law of the United States.

6. The First Amendment guarantees freedom of _____ .

7. A citizen's most important right is the right to _____ .

Down

2. A change to the Constitution is called an _____ .

3. The first ten amendments to the Constitution are the Bill of _____ .

4. A _____ of the United States must be 18 years old to vote.

The Civil War

After you finish this lesson, you will be able to talk about

★ the Civil War
★ the Confederacy and the Union
★ Abraham Lincoln
★ the Emancipation Proclamation

Words to Know

Practice saying these words.

- ★ southern
- ★ Confederate
- ★ northern
- ★ Union
- ★ slave

- ★ state's rights
- ★ divide
- ★ unite
- ★ document

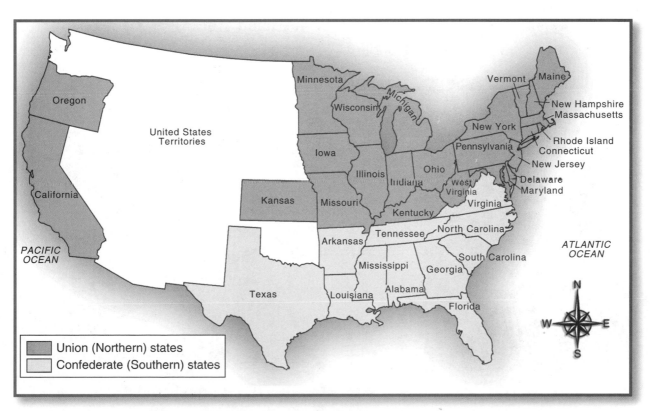

The United States in 1863

Americans fought the Civil War from 1861 to 1865. The Southern (Confederate) states wanted to leave the United States and start their own country. They fought against the Northern (Union) states.

17

Look and read.

Slaves

The Civil War was fought over slavery and state's rights. The South wanted to keep slavery. The North wanted to end slavery.

Ulysses S. Grant

The Northern states were called the Union. Ulysses S. Grant was the commander of the Union Army.

Robert E. Lee

The Southern states were called the Confederacy. Robert E. Lee was the commander of the Confederate Army.

Partner Work

Take turns. Read the sentences to your partner. Your partner writes the sentences.

See for Yourself

Can you find the Confederate states on the map on page 76? Can you find the Union states?

Talk It Over

Practice the dialogs with a partner.

A: Who was President during the Civil War?

B: Abraham Lincoln.

A: Did the Civil War divide the United States?

B: Yes, it did. The states were not united. President Lincoln wanted to keep the country united.

A: Abraham Lincoln signed the Emancipation Proclamation.

B: What's the Emancipation Proclamation?

A: It's a document that freed the slaves.

B: That's because Abraham Lincoln wanted freedom for all people.

Abraham Lincoln with Union soldiers

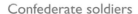

Confederate soldiers

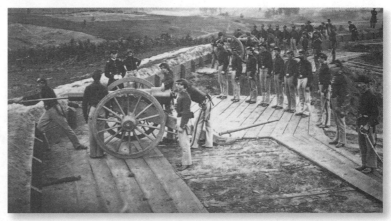

19

Figure It Out

Complete the sentences. Use the words from the box.

> Abraham Lincoln   Emancipation Proclamation
>
> Confederate   Union
>
>   slavery

1. The Southern states wanted to keep _____.

2. _____ signed the Emancipation Proclamation.

3. The _____ states were in the South.

4. The _____ freed the slaves.

5. The states in the North were called the _____.

Complete the puzzle. Use the words from the box.

> divided
> Union
> united
> Emancipation
> Civil
> Lee

Across

2. The _____ Proclamation said that many slaves were free.

5. The Civil War divided the nation. The states were not _____.

Down

1. The Civil War _____ the United States.

3. Abraham Lincoln was President during the _____ War.

4. Robert E. _____ was commander of the Confederate Army.

5. Ulysses S. Grant was commander of the _____ Army.

Lesson 4

World Wars I and II

After you finish this lesson, you will be able to talk about

★ World War I
★ the Great Depression
★ World War II
★ the United Nations

Words to Know

Practice saying these words.

★ Europe   ★ problem
★ enter   ★ provide
★ enemy   ★ economic aid
★ ally   ★ peace
★ resolve

American soldiers
during World War I

World War I began in Europe in 1914. The United States entered the war in 1917. The United States, England, France, and Russia fought against Germany and Austria-Hungary.

See for Yourself

Where would you put these countries on the map on page 77?

Talk It Over

 Practice the dialogs with a partner.

A bread line during the
Great Depression

A: What happened after World War I?

B: The Great Depression began. It was a hard time.

A: Why?

B: Many people lost their jobs, money, and homes.

American
soldiers during
World War II

A: The United States entered World War II in 1941. American soldiers
fought against Germany, Italy, and Japan. These countries were our
enemies during World War II.

B: Which countries were U.S. allies?

A: England, France, and Russia. The Allies won the war in 1945.

Read About It

Look and read.

World leaders started the United Nations after World War II. The United Nations tries to help countries resolve world problems. It also provides economic aid to many countries. Men and women from around the world meet at the United Nations to work for world peace.

The United Nations

Inside the United Nations

Group Work

Work in groups. Close the book and say the main ideas on this page in your own words.

23

Circle *true* or *false*.

1. World War I began in 1914.	true	false
2. The United States fought against Russia in World War I.	true	false
3. The Great Depression happened after World War II.	true	false
4. Many people lost their jobs during the Great Depression.	true	false
5. The United States entered World War II in 1940.	true	false
6. The United States fought against France in World War II.	true	false
7. The United Nations was started after World War II.	true	false
8. The United Nations works for world peace.	true	false

Rewrite the false sentences to make them true. There are four.

1. _____

   _____

2. _____

   _____

3. _____

   _____

4. _____

   _____

The Vietnam War

After you finish this lesson, you will be able to talk about

★ the Vietnam War
★ John F. Kennedy
★ Lyndon Johnson

Words to Know

Practice saying these words.

★ North Vietnam   ★ elect

★ Communist   ★ assassinate

★ South Vietnam   ★ protest

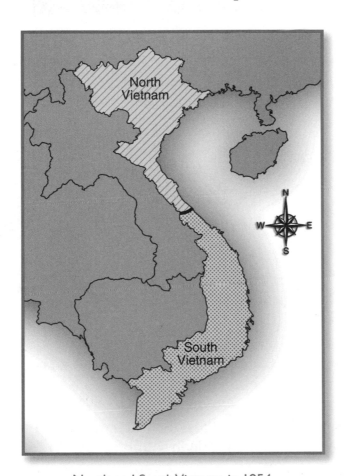

North and South Vietnam in 1954

See for Yourself

Where would you put Vietnam on the map on page 77?

In 1954 Vietnam was divided into two countries. The people of North Vietnam wanted a Communist government. The people of South Vietnam did not want to be a Communist country. The first U.S. soldiers went to help South Vietnam in 1962.

Look and read.

John F. Kennedy

John F. Kennedy was elected President in 1960. He sent the first American soldiers to Vietnam.

Lyndon Johnson becoming President

President Kennedy was assassinated in 1963. Vice President Lyndon Johnson became President. He sent more soldiers to Vietnam.

A Vietnam War protest

Some Americans wanted the United States to leave Vietnam. They protested to show they were against the war.

An American soldier returning from Vietnam in 1973

President Richard Nixon brought the American soldiers home in 1973.

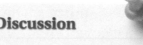

Class Discussion

Ask questions about this page. Other students answer your questions.

Figure It Out

Match.

_____ 1. Vietnam was divided into two countries in _____.

_____ 2. The United States went to war to help _____.

_____ 3. The Communist government was in _____.

_____ 4. _____ sent the first American soldiers to Vietnam.

_____ 5. President Kennedy was assassinated in _____.

_____ 6. _____ became President after President Kennedy was assassinated.

_____ 7. Some people _____ the war.

_____ 8. The American soldiers came home from Vietnam in _____.

a. protested

b. Lyndon Johnson

c. 1954

d. John F. Kennedy

e. North Vietnam

f. 1973

g. South Vietnam

h. 1963

American soldiers in Vietnam

How well did you learn the content in this unit?

Fill in the circle in front of the correct answer.

1. In what year was the Declaration of Independence adopted?
   - ○ 1757
   - ○ 1775
   - ○ 1776
   - ○ 1814

2. Which of these is guaranteed by the First Amendment?
   - ○ The right to trial by jury in most cases
   - ○ The right to bear arms
   - ○ Freedom of speech
   - ○ The right to happiness

3. What INS form is used to apply to become a naturalized citizen?
   - ○ Form N-200, Petition for Naturalization
   - ○ Form N-400, Application for Naturalization
   - ○ Social Security card
   - ○ FD-258

4. Which President freed the slaves?
   - ○ Thomas Jefferson
   - ○ Abraham Lincoln
   - ○ George Washington
   - ○ John F. Kennedy

5. Who was the first Commander in Chief of the U.S. Army and Navy?
   - ○ Thomas Jefferson
   - ○ George Washington
   - ○ Abraham Lincoln
   - ○ Patrick Henry

6. What is the Constitution?
   - ○ The Oath of Allegiance
   - ○ The House of Representatives
   - ○ The Declaration of Independence
   - ○ The supreme law of the land

7. Who was the first President of the United States?
   - ○ Abraham Lincoln
   - ○ George Washington
   - ○ Thomas Jefferson
   - ○ Patrick Henry

8. Whose rights are guaranteed by the Constitution and the Bill of Rights?
   - ○ All people living in the United States
   - ○ Registered voters
   - ○ The President
   - ○ Natural born citizens

9. What is a change to the Constitution called?
   - ○ An amendment
   - ○ Congress
   - ○ A right
   - ○ The Preamble

10. Which President created the Cabinet?
    - ○ George Washington
    - ○ Abraham Lincoln
    - ○ Ulysses S. Grant
    - ○ John F. Kennedy

11. What are the 13 original states?
   - ○ Virginia, Massachusetts, Maryland, Rhode Island, Connecticut, New Hampshire, North Carolina, South Carolina, New York, New Zealand, Pennsylvania, Delaware, Georgia
   - ○ Virginia, Massachusetts, Maryland, Rhode Island, Connecticut, New Hampshire, North Carolina, South Carolina, New York, New Jersey, Pennsylvania, Delaware, Georgia
   - ○ Virginia, Massachusetts, Maryland, Rhode Island, Connecticut, Kentucky, North Carolina, South Carolina, New York, New Jersey, Pennsylvania, Delaware, Georgia
   - ○ Virginia, Massachusetts, Maryland, Washington, D.C., Connecticut, New Hampshire, North Carolina, South Carolina, New York, New Jersey, Pennsylvania, Delaware, Georgia

12. Who was President during the Civil War?
   - ○ George Washington
   - ○ Ulysses S. Grant
   - ○ Abraham Lincoln
   - ○ Thomas Jefferson

13. What is the most important right granted to U.S. citizens?
   - ○ The right to travel with a U.S. passport
   - ○ The right to vote
   - ○ The right to apply for a federal government job
   - ○ The right to petition for close relatives to come to the United States to live

14. What is the introduction to the Constitution called?
   - ○ The First Amendment
   - ○ The Preamble
   - ○ The Bill of Rights
   - ○ The Declaration of Independence

15. What is the Bill of Rights?
   - ○ The first part of the Declaration of Independence
   - ○ The first 10 amendments to the Constitution
   - ○ The Preamble
   - ○ The Pledge of Allegiance

16. What country did the United States fight against in World War II?
   - ○ France
   - ○ Russia
   - ○ Germany
   - ○ China

17. What is one basic belief of the Declaration of Independence?
   - ○ That there are 50 states in the Union
   - ○ That all men are created equal
   - ○ That George Washington was the first President of the United States
   - ○ That the flag is red, white, and blue

18. Where does freedom of speech come from?
   - ○ The Declaration of Independence
   - ○ The President
   - ○ The Emancipation Proclamation
   - ○ The Bill of Rights

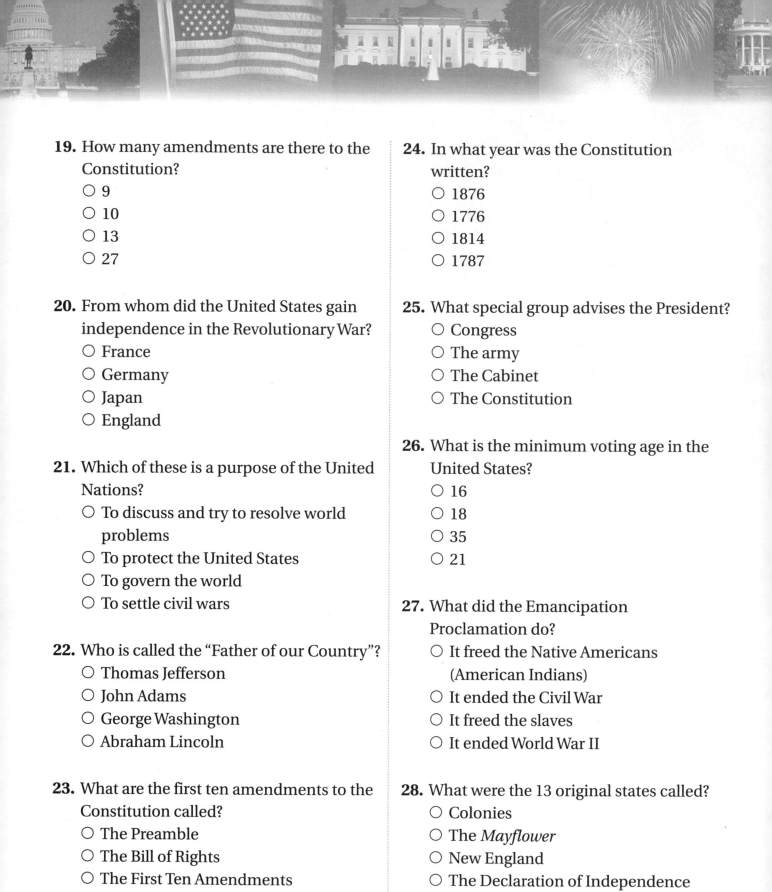

19. How many amendments are there to the Constitution?
- ○ 9
- ○ 10
- ○ 13
- ○ 27

20. From whom did the United States gain independence in the Revolutionary War?
- ○ France
- ○ Germany
- ○ Japan
- ○ England

21. Which of these is a purpose of the United Nations?
- ○ To discuss and try to resolve world problems
- ○ To protect the United States
- ○ To govern the world
- ○ To settle civil wars

22. Who is called the "Father of our Country"?
- ○ Thomas Jefferson
- ○ John Adams
- ○ George Washington
- ○ Abraham Lincoln

23. What are the first ten amendments to the Constitution called?
- ○ The Preamble
- ○ The Bill of Rights
- ○ The First Ten Amendments
- ○ The Declaration of Independence

24. In what year was the Constitution written?
- ○ 1876
- ○ 1776
- ○ 1814
- ○ 1787

25. What special group advises the President?
- ○ Congress
- ○ The army
- ○ The Cabinet
- ○ The Constitution

26. What is the minimum voting age in the United States?
- ○ 16
- ○ 18
- ○ 35
- ○ 21

27. What did the Emancipation Proclamation do?
- ○ It freed the Native Americans (American Indians)
- ○ It ended the Civil War
- ○ It freed the slaves
- ○ It ended World War II

28. What were the 13 original states called?
- ○ Colonies
- ○ The *Mayflower*
- ○ New England
- ○ The Declaration of Independence

29. Who said, "Give me liberty or give me death"?
- ○ Patrick Henry
- ○ George Washington
- ○ Thomas Jefferson
- ○ Benjamin Franklin

30. Who was the main writer of the Declaration of Independence?
- ○ George Washington
- ○ Abraham Lincoln
- ○ Patrick Henry
- ○ Thomas Jefferson

31. What is the supreme law of the United States?
- ○ The Preamble
- ○ The Bill of Rights
- ○ The Emancipation Proclamation
- ○ The Constitution

32. Which countries were our enemies during World War II?
- ○ Germany, Italy, and Japan
- ○ England, France, and Russia
- ○ North Vietnam and South Vietnam
- ○ Germany and Austria-Hungary

Talk About It

Talk about what you learned in this unit. Work with a partner. What would you like to learn more about? Make a list.

_____

_____

_____

_____

_____

_____

_____

_____

Share one idea with the class.

Unit 2

1789
Congress meets
for the first time

1800
John Adams is the first President
to move into the White House

1791
The Bill of Rights becomes
part of the Constitution

1860
Abraham Lincoln
becomes President

U.S. Government

What do you know about the government of the United States?

★ **What are the three branches of the U.S. government?**

★ **What branch makes the laws?**

★ **What are the two major political parties?**

1945
The United Nations
is created

1981
Sandra Day O'Connor
is the first woman
Supreme Court justice

1959
Alaska and Hawaii become
the 49th and 50th states

33

Lesson 6

The Legislative Branch

After you finish this lesson, you will be able to talk about

★ the legislative branch
★ Congress
★ the House of Representatives
★ the Senate

Words to Know

Practice saying these words.

★ branch
★ legislative
★ executive
★ judicial
★ elect
★ senator
★ representative

★ federal
★ declare war
★ the Capitol building
★ serve
★ Vice President
★ Speaker of the House
★ naturalized citizen

Congress makes the laws.

 The Constitution set up the U.S. government in three branches—the legislative, the executive, and the judicial. The legislative branch makes laws. Another name for the legislative branch is Congress.

34

Look and read.

President Kennedy speaking to Congress in 1963

The two parts of Congress are the Senate and the House of Representatives. Congress is elected by the citizens of the United States.

A representative at work in her office

Senators work in the Senate. There are 100 senators. Representatives work in the House of Representatives. There are 435 representatives.

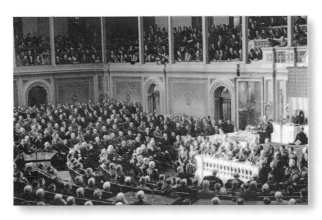

The U.S. entered World War II after Congress declared war in 1941.

Congress makes the federal laws of the United States. Congress can also declare war.

The U.S. Capitol building

Congress meets in the Capitol building. The Capitol building is in Washington, D.C.

Partner Work

Take turns. Read the sentences to your partner. Your partner writes the sentences.

See for Yourself

Can you find Washington, D.C., on the map on page 76?

Write the sentences.

1. There are 100 senators in Congress. Each state elects two.

   _____

   _____

2. There are 435 voting members in the House of Representatives.

   _____

   _____

3. A senator can serve in Congress for six years. A representative can serve for two years.

   _____

   _____

4. A senator must be at least 30 years old. A representative must be at least 25 years old.

   _____

   _____

5. The Vice President is the leader of the Senate. The Speaker of the House is the leader of the House of Representatives.

   _____

   _____

   _____

Partner Work

Take turns. Read the sentences to your partner. Your partner writes the sentences.

Figure It Out

Complete the chart. Use the numbers from the box.

25	2	6	100
2	30	435	

Congress

The House of Representatives

1. _____ representatives

2. Elected every _____ years

   There is no limit to how often he or she can be re-elected.

3. Must be a citizen—either born in the U.S. or naturalized

4. Must be at least _____ years old

The Senate

1. Each state elects _____ senators = _____ senators

2. Elected every _____ years

   There is no limit to how often he or she can be re-elected.

3. Must be a citizen—either born in the U.S. or naturalized

4. Must be at least _____ years old

Inside the U.S. Capitol building

Lesson 7

The Executive Branch

After you finish this lesson, you will be able to talk about

★ the executive branch
★ the President
★ the Vice President

 Words to Know

Practice saying these words.

★ head
★ enforce
★ the electoral college
★ official
★ the White House

★ sign bills into law
★ veto
★ inaugurate
★ term
★ requirement

President George W. Bush
in his office in the White House

 The President, the Cabinet, and departments under the Cabinet members are the executive branch of the U.S. government. The President is the head of the executive branch. The executive branch enforces the law.

38

Read About It

Look and read.

President Bush and Vice President
Cheney were elected together.

The electoral college elects the
President. The Vice President is elected
with the President.

The White House

The President's official home is the
White House. The White House is located
at 1600 Pennsylvania Avenue, in
Washington, D.C.

President Johnson signing
the Civil Rights Act of 1964

The President signs bills into law and also
vetoes bills. The President is Commander in
Chief of the U.S. military.

Vice President Lyndon Johnson became
President when John Kennedy was assassinated.

If the President dies, the Vice President
becomes President. If both the President and
the Vice President die, the Speaker of the
House becomes President.

Group Work

Work in groups. Close the book and say the
main ideas on this page in your own words.

39

Talk It Over

Practice the dialogs with a partner.

A: For how long is the President elected?

B: Four years.

A: When do we vote for the President?

B: In November.

A: When is the President inaugurated?

B: In January.

George Washington's inauguration

A: How many full terms can the President serve?

B: Two terms, or eight years.

A: What are some of the requirements to be President?

B: The President must be at least 35 years old, must be a natural born citizen, and must have lived in the United States for at least 14 years.

Figure It Out

Complete the chart. Make a ✓.

	The President	The Vice President
1. becomes President if the President dies		
2. is the Commander in Chief of the U.S. military		
3. heads the executive branch of the government		
4. is elected with the President		
5. lives in the White House		

35   November   4   14   January   2

Complete the sentences. Use the words from the box to answer 1–6.

1. The President is elected for _____ years.

2. The President may serve _____ full terms.

3. The President must be at least _____ years old.

4. The President must have lived in the United States for at least

   _____ years.

5. The President is elected in _____ .

6. The President is inaugurated in _____ .

7. The current President is _____ .

8. The current Vice President is _____ .

41

The Judicial Branch

After you finish this lesson, you will be able to talk about

* ★ the judicial branch
* ★ the Supreme Court

Words to Know

Practice saying these words.

* ★ justice
* ★ interpret
* ★ agree
* ★ decision

* ★ final
* ★ choose
* ★ nominate
* ★ approve

Visitors waiting outside the Supreme Court Building

The Supreme Court is the highest part of the judicial branch of the U.S. government. The nine Supreme Court justices interpret and explain the law. They make sure that the laws agree with the Constitution. The Chief Justice is the head of the Supreme Court.

42

Talk It Over

Practice the dialogs with a partner.

A: The Supreme Court is the highest court in the United States, right?

B: Yes, the decisions of the Supreme Court justices are final.

A: How are the justices chosen?

B: The President nominates the justices, and Congress approves them.

The nine justices of the Supreme Court

A: How many justices are there?

B: Nine, including the Chief Justice.

A: Who's the current Chief Justice?

B: William Rehnquist.

Chief Justice William Rehnquist

Write It Down

Write the sentences.

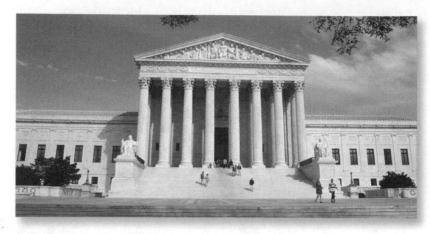

The Supreme Court Building

1. The three branches of the U.S. government are the legislative, executive, and judicial branches.

   _____

   _____

2. The Supreme Court is the highest part of the judicial branch. It is the highest court in the United States.

   _____

   _____

3. The justices decide if the laws agree with the Constitution. The decisions of the Supreme Court are final.

   _____

   _____

4. There are nine Supreme Court justices. William Rehnquist is the Chief Justice. He is the head of the Supreme Court.

   _____

   _____

Partner Work

Take turns. Read the sentences to your partner. Your partner writes the sentences.

Figure It Out

Complete the sentences. Use the words from the box.

> Congress   Chief Justice
> Supreme Court   President

1. The _____ decides if the laws agree with the Constitution.

2. The _____ is the head of the Supreme Court.

3. The _____ nominates the Supreme Court justices.

4. _____ approves the Supreme Court justices.

Complete the chart. Write the branch of government. Use the words from the box.

> Judicial   Legislative   Executive

The Three Branches of U.S. Government
1. _____ Enforces the laws The President is the head.
2. _____ Makes the laws The Senate and the House of Representatives
3. _____ Interprets the law Has nine justices

45

States and Capitals

After you finish this lesson, you will be able to talk about

★ the U.S. government
★ federal and state levels of government
★ capital cities

 Words to Know

Practice saying these words.

★ own

★ make laws

★ capital

The New York state legislature meets in this building in Albany, New York.

 There are fifty states in the United States. Each state has its own government. Each state government can make its own laws. But these laws must agree with the U.S. Constitution. Most state governments have three branches— legislative, executive, and judicial.

Read About It

Look and read.

Denali National Park, Alaska

Alaska became the 49th state on January 3, 1959.

Kailua Beach, Hawaii

Hawaii became the 50th state on August 21, 1959.

Complete the sentences. Write about the state you live in.

1. The name of the state I live in is _____ .

2. The capital of my state is _____ .

3. The two senators from my state are _____ and _____ .

4. The governor is the head executive of a state government. The governor of my state is

   _____ .

5. The mayor is the head executive of a city government. The mayor of my city is

   _____ .

See for Yourself

Can you find your state on the map on page 76?
Can you find Alaska or Hawaii?

47

Read About It

Look and read. Then circle your state and state capital.

The government of each state is in the state capital.

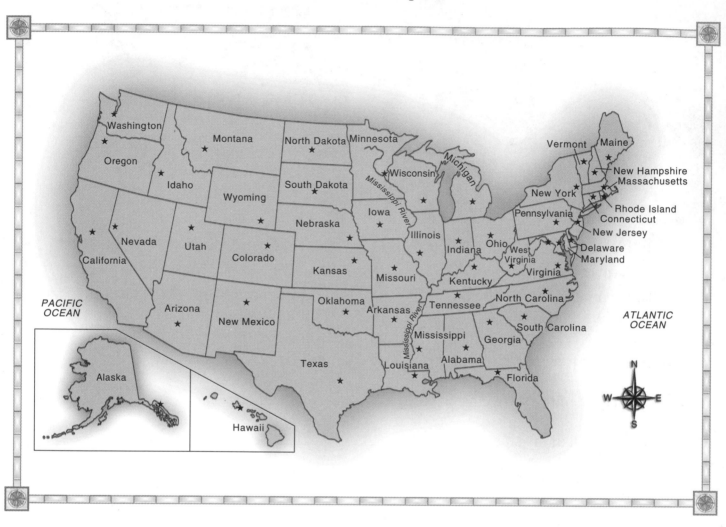

Map Key

State	State Capital
Alabama	★ Montgomery
Alaska	★ Juneau
Arizona	★ Phoenix
Arkansas	★ Little Rock
California	★ Sacramento
Colorado	★ Denver
Connecticut	★ Hartford
Delaware	★ Dover
Florida	★ Tallahassee
Georgia	★ Atlanta
Hawaii	★ Honolulu
Idaho	★ Boise
Illinois	★ Springfield
Indiana	★ Indianapolis
Iowa	★ Des Moines
Kansas	★ Topeka
Kentucky	★ Frankfort
Louisiana	★ Baton Rouge
Maine	★ Augusta
Maryland	★ Annapolis
Massachusetts	★ Boston
Michigan	★ Lansing
Minnesota	★ St. Paul
Mississippi	★ Jackson
Missouri	★ Jefferson City
Montana	★ Helena
Nebraska	★ Lincoln
Nevada	★ Carson City
New Hampshire	★ Concord
New Jersey	★ Trenton
New Mexico	★ Santa Fe
New York	★ Albany
North Carolina	★ Raleigh
North Dakota	★ Bismarck
Ohio	★ Columbus
Oklahoma	★ Oklahoma City
Oregon	★ Salem
Pennsylvania	★ Harrisburg
Rhode Island	★ Providence
South Carolina	★ Columbia
South Dakota	★ Pierre
Tennessee	★ Nashville
Texas	★ Austin
Utah	★ Salt Lake City
Vermont	★ Montpelier
Virginia	★ Richmond
Washington	★ Olympia
West Virginia	★ Charleston
Wisconsin	★ Madison
Wyoming	★ Cheyenne

48

Figure It Out

Plan a trip. Below is the map of your trip. Look at the map on page 48 to find the names of the cities and states you will be visiting. Write the names on the lines below.

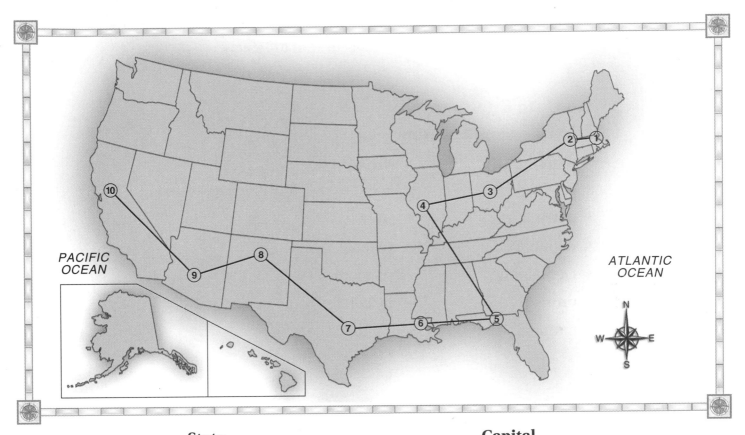

	State	Capital
1.		
2.		
3.		
4.		
5.		
6.		
7.		
8.		
9.		
10.		

The U.S. Political System

After you finish this lesson, you will be able to talk about

★ the two main political parties
★ your local and state government officials

Words to Know

Practice saying these words.

★ republic
★ political
★ party
★ Republican
★ Democratic
★ protect
★ national

★ convention
★ policy
★ governor
★ mayor
★ city manager
★ city council
★ municipal court

Americans vote for their leaders.

The United States is a republic. In a republican form of government, the people elect their leaders. These leaders make laws for the people and lead the government.

Look and read.

The Republican and Democratic candidates for President in 2000

There are two major political parties in the United States. They are the Republican and the Democratic parties. The parties want to work for and protect the country. They both work on the national, state, and local levels.

The Democratic national convention in 2000

Every four years the Democrats and Republicans have large meetings called conventions. The parties decide on their leaders and policies at these conventions.

Class Discussion

Ask questions about this page. Other students answer your questions.

51

Write It Down

Federal, state, and city governments have three branches.
Complete the chart. Use the names of the people who hold these offices today.

FEDERAL

Executive Branch	Legislative Branch	Judicial Branch
President: _____	Senators: _____ _____	Chief Justice: _____
Vice President: _____	Representative(s): _____	
Party: _____		

STATE _____ (your state)

Executive Branch	Legislative Branch	Judicial Branch
Governor: _____	State Senators: _____ _____	Chief Justice: _____
Party: _____	Representative:	

CITY _____ (your city)

Executive Branch	Legislative Branch	Judicial Branch
Mayor or City manager: _____	City Council	Municipal courts

Figure It Out

Complete the chart. Where can you find this person? Make a ✓.

	Federal Government	State Government	Local Government
1. Governor			
2. Municipal Court Judge			
3. President			
4. Chief Justice			
5. Mayor			

Complete the sentences. Circle the answer. Then write the sentence.

1. The form of government in the United States is a (republic, policy).

   _____

   _____

2. There are (two, three) major political parties in the United States.

   _____

   _____

3. One is the Democratic party. One is the (Republican, Executive) party.

   _____

   _____

4. The three (parties, branches) of the U.S. government are the legislative, the executive, and the judicial.

   _____

   _____

U.S. Government Unit Checkup

How well did you learn the content in this unit?

Fill in the circle in front of the correct answer.

1. Who is the Chief Justice of the Supreme Court today?
   - ○ George W. Bush
   - ○ William Rehnquist
   - ○ Thomas Jefferson
   - ○ Dick Cheney

2. What is the highest court in the United States?
   - ○ The Constitution
   - ○ The President
   - ○ Congress
   - ○ The Supreme Court

3. What are the three branches of our government?
   - ○ Democratic, Republican, Independent
   - ○ Department of Justice, Department of State, Department of Defense
   - ○ Executive, Judicial, Legislative
   - ○ Police, Education, Legislative

4. What is the U.S. Capitol?
   - ○ Where the President lives
   - ○ Where Congress meets
   - ○ Where the Cabinet meets
   - ○ Where the Supreme Court meets

5. What are the duties of the Supreme Court?
   - ○ To serve the President as Cabinet members
   - ○ To write laws
   - ○ To interpret and explain laws
   - ○ To execute laws

6. Why are there 100 senators in the Senate?
   - ○ Because that is all that fits in the Senate Gallery
   - ○ Because it must have half the number of representatives
   - ○ Tradition
   - ○ Each state elects 2

7. Who elects Congress?
   - ○ The electoral college
   - ○ The citizens of the United States
   - ○ The President
   - ○ The governor

8. In what month do we vote for the President?
   - ○ January
   - ○ July
   - ○ June
   - ○ November

9. How many branches are there in our government?
   - ○ 2
   - ○ 3
   - ○ 4
   - ○ 6

10. What are the 49th and 50th states of the Union?
   - ○ Alaska and Hawaii
   - ○ Hawaii and Puerto Rico
   - ○ Puerto Rico and Guam
   - ○ Alaska and Puerto Rico

11. What is the name of the President's home?
   ○ The U.S. Capitol
   ○ The White House
   ○ The "Star-Spangled Banner"
   ○ The *Mayflower*

12. Where is the White House located?
   ○ In Philadelphia
   ○ In New York City
   ○ In Washington, D.C., at 1600 Pennsylvania Avenue
   ○ In Washington, D.C., across from the Capitol

13. Who becomes President if the President and the Vice President die?
   ○ The Speaker of the House of Representatives
   ○ The Senate Majority Leader
   ○ The Chairman of the Joint Chiefs of Staff
   ○ The Chief Justice of the Supreme Court

14. Who is the Commander in Chief of the U.S. military?
   ○ The President
   ○ The Chief Justice of the Supreme Court
   ○ The Vice President
   ○ The Speaker of the House of Representatives

15. What is the legislative branch of our government?
   ○ Congress
   ○ The Supreme Court
   ○ The presidency
   ○ The House of Representatives

16. How many Supreme Court justices are there?
   ○ 3
   ○ 9
   ○ 10
   ○ 13

17. Who is the President of the United States today?
   ○ Bill Clinton
   ○ George W. Bush
   ○ Dick Cheney
   ○ Al Gore

18. Which of the following is not a Constitutional requirement to be eligible to be President?
   ○ Must be at least 35 years old by the time he/she will serve
   ○ Must have lived in the United States for at least 14 years
   ○ Must have served as a governor
   ○ Must be a natural born citizen of the United States

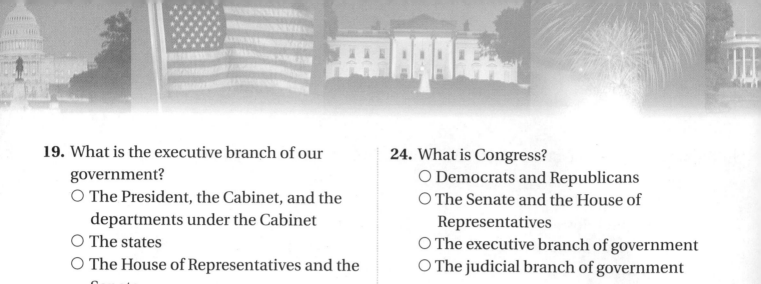

19. What is the executive branch of our government?
    ○ The President, the Cabinet, and the departments under the Cabinet
    ○ The states
    ○ The House of Representatives and the Senate
    ○ The Supreme Court

20. What are the two major political parties in the United States?
    ○ The House of Representatives and the Senate
    ○ The President and the Vice President
    ○ Democratic and Republican
    ○ Congress and the Supreme Court

21. Who nominates Supreme Court justices?
    ○ The electoral college
    ○ The President
    ○ The Senate
    ○ The people

22. Who signs bills into law?
    ○ The Supreme Court
    ○ Congress
    ○ The President
    ○ The Senate

23. How many senators are there in Congress?
    ○ 50
    ○ 100
    ○ 102
    ○ 435

24. What is Congress?
    ○ Democrats and Republicans
    ○ The Senate and the House of Representatives
    ○ The executive branch of government
    ○ The judicial branch of government

25. Who makes the laws in the United States?
    ○ The President
    ○ The Speaker of the House
    ○ The Chief Justice of the Supreme Court
    ○ Congress

26. In what month is the new President inaugurated?
    ○ July
    ○ September
    ○ November
    ○ January

27. Who elects the President?
    ○ The electoral college
    ○ The Senate
    ○ Congress
    ○ The Cabinet

28. Who has the power to declare war?
    ○ The President
    ○ The Vice President
    ○ Congress
    ○ The Chief Justice of the Supreme Court

29. For how long do we elect the President?
- ○ 2 years
- ○ There is no limit
- ○ 4 years
- ○ 6 years

30. Who becomes the President if the President dies?
- ○ One of the senators
- ○ The Chief Justice
- ○ The leader of the Cabinet
- ○ The Vice President

31. What is the head executive of a state government called?
- ○ Speaker of the House
- ○ Governor
- ○ Vice President
- ○ Mayor

32. How many terms can a President serve?
- ○ 2
- ○ 3
- ○ 4
- ○ 9

Talk About It

Talk about what you learned in this unit. Work with a partner.
What would you like to learn more about? Make a list.

_____

_____

_____

_____

_____

_____

_____

_____

_____

Share one idea with the class.

Unit 3

January
Martin Luther King, Jr. Day

May
Memorial Day

February
Presidents' Day

June
Flag Day

U.S.
Celebrations

**What do you know about celebrations
in the United States?**

★ **What was the first American holiday?**

★ **Why is July 4 an important day for Americans?**

★ **What is the "Star-Spangled Banner"?**

★ **What do the stars and stripes on the flag mean?**

July
Independence Day

November
Veteran's Day

September
Labor Day

November
Thanksgiving

Lesson 11

Thanksgiving

After you finish this lesson, you will be able to talk about

★ the Pilgrims and Native Americans
★ Thanksgiving

Words to Know

Practice saying these words.

★ holiday   ★ plant
★ celebrate   ★ corn
★ sail   ★ hunt
★ gain   ★ fish
★ religious freedom ★ harvest
★ the *Mayflower*   ★ meal

A Thanksgiving celebration

Thanksgiving was the first American holiday. Americans celebrate Thanksgiving on the fourth Thursday in November. On Thanksgiving Day Americans give thanks for the good things in their lives. They share a special meal with their family and friends.

Read About It

Look and read.

The *Mayflower*

In 1620 a group of people sailed from England to gain religious freedom. The people were Pilgrims. Their ship was the *Mayflower*.

Winter was hard for the Pilgrims.

The first winter in America was hard for the Pilgrims. They had little food. Native Americans helped the Pilgrims plant corn and hunt and fish. To celebrate the first harvest, the Pilgrims and the Native Americans shared a large meal.

Group Work

Work in groups. Close the book and say the main ideas on this page in your own words.

61

Figure It Out

Complete the puzzle. Use the words from the box.

Mayflower   Native Americans   November
meal   Pilgrims   freedom

Across

2. _____ helped the Pilgrims.
4. The _____ left England in 1620.
5. The Pilgrims left England to find religious _____.

Down

1. After the harvest, they had a large _____.
2. Americans celebrate Thanksgiving in _____.
3. The Pilgrims came to America on the _____.

The first Thanksgiving

Lesson 12

Independence Day

After you finish this lesson you, will be able to talk about

★ Independence Day
★ Francis Scott Key and the "Star-Spangled Banner"
★ the U.S. flag

Words to Know

Practice saying these words.

★ picnic
★ parade
★ fly the flag
★ song

★ national anthem
★ star
★ stripe

An Independence Day parade

 We celebrate Independence Day on the Fourth of July. On this day, Americans remember the signing of the Declaration of Independence on July 4, 1776. People have picnics and parades and fly the flag.

Practice the dialog with a partner.

A Fourth of July celebration in New York City

A: What do Americans celebrate on July 4?

B: They celebrate Independence Day.

A: Why is Independence Day important?

B: On July 4, 1776 leaders of the thirteen colonies signed the Declaration of Independence and the colonies became independent from England.

Read About It

 Look and read.

Francis Scott Key

Francis Scott Key wrote the "Star-Spangled Banner" in 1814. This song is about the U.S. flag.

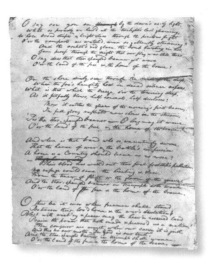

The "Star-Spangled Banner"

The "Star-Spangled Banner" is the national anthem of the United States.

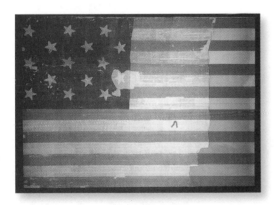

The U.S. flag in 1814

The U.S. flag is red, white, and blue. The stars are white. The stripes are red and white.

The U.S. flag today

Today the flag has fifty stars and thirteen stripes. There is a star for every state in the Union. There is a stripe for each of the first thirteen states.

Class Discussion

Ask questions about this page. Other students answer your questions.

See for Yourself

If you are interested in learning more about the "Star-Spangled Banner," turn to page 75.

Write the sentences.

The U.S. flag in 1777

1. The United States began with thirteen colonies.

   _____

   _____

2. The flag has thirteen stripes, one stripe for each of the first states.

   _____

   _____

3. Now the United States has fifty states.

   _____

   _____

4. The flag has fifty stars, one star for each state.

   _____

   _____

Partner Work

Take turns. Read the sentences to your partner. Your partner writes the sentences.

Figure It Out

Complete the puzzle. Use the words from the box.

July
parade
Union
stripe
Banner
Declaration

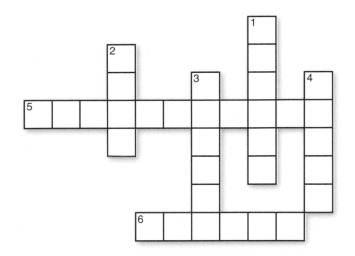

Across

5. Americans remember the signing of the _____ of Independence on the Fourth of July.

6. Many cities celebrate Independence Day with a _____.

Down

1. There is a _____ on the flag for each of the thirteen colonies.

2. _____ 4 is America's birthday.

3. The "Star-Spangled _____" was written by Francis Scott Key.

4. There is a star on the flag for every state in the _____.

Complete the sentences. Use the words from the puzzle.

1. There are thirteen _____s on the flag.

2. Today there are fifty states in the _____.

3. _____ is another word for flag.

4. Independence Day is in _____.

5. Americans celebrate the Fourth of July with picnics and

_____s.

6. Thomas Jefferson wrote the _____ of

Independence.

67

Other Holidays

After you finish this lesson, you will be able to talk about

★ Presidents' Day
★ Flag Day
★ Labor Day
★ Memorial Day
★ Martin Luther King, Jr. Day

Words to Know

Practice saying these words.

★ get time off   ★ symbol
★ honor   ★ civil rights
★ worker   ★ win

Americans enjoy celebrating holidays with their families.

American holidays honor special people or times in U.S. history. Banks and schools often close. Many people get time off from work and school.

Read About It

Look and read.

George Washington and Abraham Lincoln

Presidents' Day honors two great Presidents, George Washington and Abraham Lincoln. Presidents' Day is the third Monday in February.

A Labor Day parade honoring American workers

Labor Day honors American workers. Labor Day is the first Monday in September.

Houses decorated for Flag Day

On Flag Day Americans remember that the flag is our national symbol. Flag Day is June 14.

The Vietnam War Memorial honors the Americans who died in that war.

On Memorial Day we remember the men and women who died in war. Memorial Day is the last Monday in May.

Partner Work

Take turns. Read the sentences to your partner. Your partner writes the sentences.

69

Look and read.

Martin Luther King, Jr. speaking in Washington, D.C. in 1963

Martin Luther King, Jr. in his office in 1966

Martin Luther King, Jr. was a civil rights leader. He helped black Americans win the rights guaranteed to them in the Constitution. Dr. King worked hard to change laws that were not fair. His birthday is a national holiday and is celebrated on the third Monday in January.

Figure It Out

Circle the dates of these holidays.

Flag Day   Independence Day   Labor Day
Memorial Day   Martin Luther King, Jr. Day   Presidents' Day

January

Sun	Mon	Tue	Wed	Thu	Fri	Sat
		1	2	3	4	5
6	7	8	9	10	11	12
13	14	15	16	17	18	19
20	21	22	23	24	25	26
27	28	29	30	31		

February

Sun	Mon	Tue	Wed	Thu	Fri	Sat
					1	2
3	4	5	6	7	8	9
10	11	12	13	14	15	16
17	18	19	20	21	22	23
24	25	26	27	28		

May

Sun	Mon	Tue	Wed	Thu	Fri	Sat
			1	2	3	4
5	6	7	8	9	10	11
12	13	14	15	16	17	18
19	20	21	22	23	24	25
26	27	28	29	30	31	

June

Sun	Mon	Tue	Wed	Thu	Fri	Sat
						1
2	3	4	5	6	7	8
9	10	11	12	13	14	15
16	17	18	19	20	21	22
23/30	24	25	26	27	28	29

July

Sun	Mon	Tue	Wed	Thu	Fri	Sat
	1	2	3	4	5	6
7	8	9	10	11	12	13
14	15	16	17	18	19	20
21	22	23	24	25	26	27
28	29	30	31			

September

Sun	Mon	Tue	Wed	Thu	Fri	Sat
1	2	3	4	5	6	7
8	9	10	11	12	13	14
15	16	17	18	19	20	21
22	23	24	25	26	27	28
29	30					

U.S. Celebrations Unit Checkup

How well did you learn the content in this unit?

Fill in the circle in front of the correct answer.

1. How many stripes are there on the flag?
   - ○ 13
   - ○ 51
   - ○ 10
   - ○ 50

2. What is the name of the ship that brought the Pilgrims to America?
   - ○ The *Nina*
   - ○ The Bill of Rights
   - ○ The *Mayflower*
   - ○ The *Santa Maria*

3. How many states are there in the Union?
   - ○ 40
   - ○ 51
   - ○ 52
   - ○ 50

4. Who helped the Pilgrims in America?
   - ○ Native Americans/American Indians
   - ○ The governor
   - ○ George Washington
   - ○ Christopher Columbus

5. Who was Martin Luther King, Jr. ?
   - ○ A Republican leader
   - ○ A Pilgrim leader
   - ○ A civil rights leader
   - ○ A governor

6. What is the national anthem of the United States?
   - ○ The Constitution
   - ○ The Bill of Rights
   - ○ The "Star-Spangled Banner"
   - ○ The Declaration of Independence

7. What color are the stripes on the American flag?
   - ○ Red and white
   - ○ Red and blue
   - ○ Blue and white
   - ○ White

8. What do the stripes on the flag represent?
   - ○ One for each state
   - ○ One for each amendment to the Constitution
   - ○ The Cabinet
   - ○ The first 13 states

9. Why did the Pilgrims come to America?
   - ○ To meet Native Americans/ American Indians
   - ○ To find gold
   - ○ To gain religious freedom
   - ○ To celebrate Thanksgiving

10. How many stars are there on our flag?
    - ○ 50
    - ○ 51
    - ○ 100
    - ○ 52

11. Independence Day celebrates independence from whom?
   ○ France
   ○ England
   ○ Germany
   ○ Japan

12. What do the stars on the flag mean?
   ○ One for each President
   ○ One for each amendment to the Constitution
   ○ They don't mean anything
   ○ One for each state

13. Who wrote the "Star-Spangled Banner?"
   ○ George Washington
   ○ Patrick Henry
   ○ Thomas Jefferson
   ○ Francis Scott Key

14. What do we celebrate on the Fourth of July ?
   ○ Flag Day
   ○ Independence Day
   ○ Presidents' Day
   ○ Veterans' Day

15. What holiday was celebrated for the first time by the American colonists?
   ○ Independence Day
   ○ Memorial Day
   ○ Thanksgiving
   ○ Labor Day

16. What is the date of Independence Day?
   ○ January 1
   ○ July 1
   ○ July 4
   ○ The first Monday in September

Talk About It

Talk about what you learned in this unit. Work with a partner.
What would you like to learn more about? Make a list.

_____

_____

_____

_____

_____

_____

_____

_____

Share one idea with the class.

About the Bill of Rights

The Bill of Rights is the first ten amendments to the Constitution. The Bill of Rights guarantees the following:

Amendment 1 Freedom of Religion, Speech, Press, Assembly, and Petition
* ★ People can practice any religion they want, or no religion at all.
* ★ People can say what they believe to be true.
* ★ People can write and print what they believe to be true.
* ★ People can meet in groups in a peaceful way and for peaceful reasons.
* ★ People can ask the government to change something they think is wrong.

Amendment 2 The Right to Bear Arms
* ★ People can own guns (with some restrictions).

Amendment 3 The Housing of Soldiers
* ★ The government cannot make people keep soldiers in their homes during peacetime.

Amendment 4 Search and Arrest
* ★ The government cannot search people's homes or arrest people without a warrant.

Amendment 5 The Rights of Accused Persons
* ★ People cannot be tried twice for the same crime. They also have the right to refuse to testify against themselves.

Amendment 6 The Right to a Fair Trial
* ★ People accused of a crime have the right to a speedy, public, and fair trial. They also have the right to a lawyer.

Amendment 7 Civil Cases
* ★ People have the right to a jury trial in most civil cases.

Amendment 8 Bail and Punishment
* ★ People cannot be asked to pay very high fines or be given cruel or unusual punishment.

Amendment 9 Other Rights
* ★ People have rights not listed in the Constitution. These rights must be protected by the government.

Amendment 10 Powers Belonging to States
* ★ Any powers that the Constitution did not give to the federal government belong to the state governments or to the people.

The Star-Spangled Banner

The "Star-Spangled Banner" is the national anthem of the United States.
It was written by Francis Scott Key.

Oh! say, can you see, by the dawn's early light,

What so proudly we hailed at the twilight's last gleaming?

Whose broad stripes and bright stars, through the perilous fight,

O'er the ramparts we watched were so gallantly streaming?

And the rockets' red glare, the bombs bursting in air,

Gave proof through the night that our flag was still there.

Oh! say, does that star-spangled banner yet wave,

O'er the land of the free and the home of the brave?

The United States

PACIFIC OCEAN

Alaska

Hawaii

Washington

Oregon

California

Nevada

Idaho

Montana

Arizona

Utah

Wyoming

North Dakota

New Mexico

Colorado

South Dakota

Minnesota

Nebraska

Texas

Kansas

Iowa

Wisconsin

Oklahoma

Missouri

Mississippi River

Mississippi River

Michigan

Louisiana

Arkansas

Illinois

Indiana

Mississippi River

Mississippi

Tennessee

Kentucky

Ohio

West Virginia

Pennsylvania

New York

Vermont

Maine

Alabama

Georgia

North Carolina

Virginia

New Hampshire

Florida

South Carolina

Washington, D.C.

Maryland

Delaware

New Jersey

Connecticut

Rhode Island

Massachusetts

ATLANTIC OCEAN

N W S E

The World

Asia

INDIAN
OCEAN

Europe

Africa

ATLANTIC
OCEAN

South
America

North
America

Antarctica

PACIFIC
OCEAN

Asia

Australia

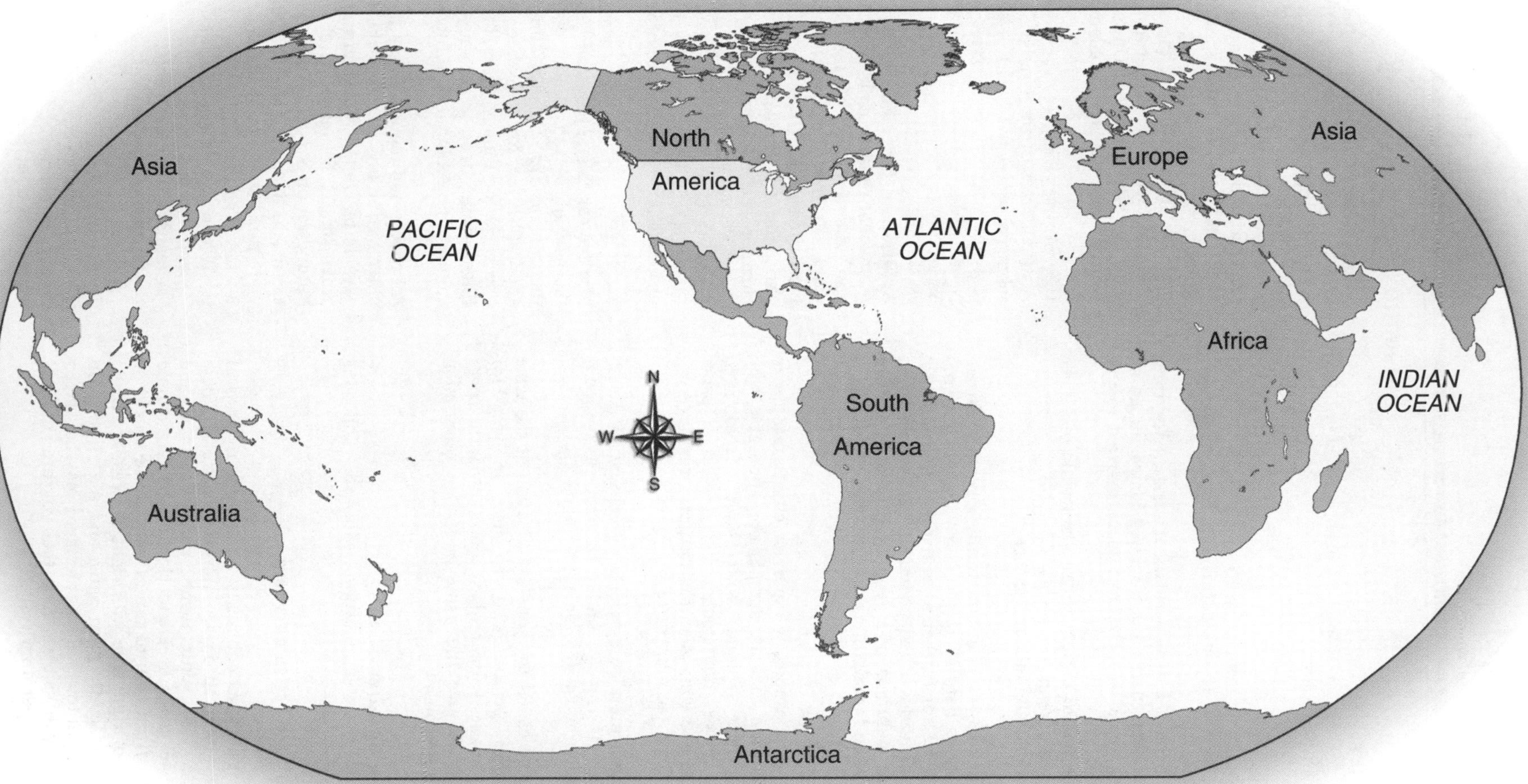

INSTRUCTIONS

Purpose of This Form.
This form is for use to apply to become a naturalized citizen of the United States.

Who May File.
You may apply for naturalization if:

- you have been a lawful permanent resident for five years;
- you have been a lawful permanent resident for three years, have been married to a United States citizen for those three years, and continue to be married to that U.S. citizen;
- you are the lawful permanent resident child of United States citizen parents; or
- you have qualifying military service.

Children under 18 may automatically become citizens when their parents naturalize. You may inquire at your local Service office for further information. If you do not meet the qualifications listed above but believe that you are eligible for naturalization, you may inquire at your local Service office for additional information.

General Instructions.
Please answer all questions by typing or clearly printing in black ink. Indicate that an item is not applicable with "N/A". If an answer is "none," write "none". If you need extra space to answer any item, attach a sheet of paper with your name and your alien registration number (A #), if any, and indicate the number of the item.

Every application must be properly signed and filed with the correct fee. If you are under 18 years of age, your parent or guardian must sign the application.

If you wish to be called for your examination at the same time as another person who is also applying for naturalization, make your request on a separate cover sheet. Be sure to give the name and alien registration number of that person.

Initial Evidence Requirements.
You must file your application with the following evidence:

A copy of your alien registration card.

Photographs. You must submit two color photographs of yourself taken within 30 days of this application. These photos must be glossy, unretouched and unmounted, and have a white background. Dimension of the face should be about 1 inch from chin to top of hair. Face should be 3/4 frontal view of right side with right ear visible. Using pencil or felt pen, lightly print name and A #, if any, on the back of each photo. This requirement may be waived by the Service if you can establish that you are confined because of age or physical infirmity.

Fingerprints. If you are between the ages of 14 and 75 years of age, you must be fingerprinted in connection with this application. *Applications residing in the United States.* After filing the application, INS will notify you in writing of the time and location where you must go to be fingerprinted. Failure to appear to be fingerprinted may result in denial of the application. *Applicants residing Abroad.* A completed fingerprint card (Form FD-258) must be submitted with the application. Do not bend, fold, or crease the fingerprint card. Fingerprint cards must be prepared by a United States consular office or United States military installation.

U.S. Military Service. If you have ever served in the Armed Forces of the United States at any time, you must submit a completed Form G-325B. If your application is based on your military service you must also submit Form N-426, "Request for Certification of Military or Naval Service."

Application for Child. If this application is for a permanent resident child of U.S. citizen parents, you must also submit copies of the child's birth certificate, the parents' marriage certificate, and evidence of the parents' U.S. citizenship. If the parents are divorced, you must also submit the divorce decree and evidence that the citizen parent has legal custody of the child.

Where to File.
File this application at the local Service office having jurisdiction over your place of residence.

Fee.
The fee for this application is $225. If you are between the ages of 14 and 75 and residing in the United States, there is a $25 fingerprinting fee in addition to the application fee, for a total fee of $250. You may submit one check or money order for both the application and fingerprinting fees. Fees must be submitted in the exact amount. Fees cannot be refunded. **DO NOT MAIL CASH.**

All checks and money orders must be drawn on a bank or other institution located in the United States and must be payable in United States currency. The check or money order should be made payable to the Immigration and Naturalization Service, except that:

- If you live in Guam, and are filing this application in Guam, make your check or money order payable to the "Treasurer, Guam."
- If you live in the Virgin Islands, and are filing this application in the Virgin Islands, make your check or money order payable to the "Commissioner of Finance of the Virgin Islands."

Checks are accepted subject to collection. An uncollected check will render the application and any document issued invalid. A charge of $30.00 will be imposed if a check in payment of a fee is not honored by the bank on which it is drawn.

Form N-400 (Rev. 01/15/99)N

Processing Information.

Rejection. Any application that is not signed or is not accompanied by the proper fee will be rejected with a notice that the application is deficient. You may correct the deficiency and resubmit the application. However, an application is not considered properly filed until it is accepted by the Service.

Requests for more information. We may request more information or evidence. We may also request that you submit the originals of any copy. We will return these originals when they are no longer required.

Interview. After you file your application, you will be notified to appear at a Service office to be examined under oath or affirmation. This interview may not be waived. If you are an adult, you must show that you have a knowledge and understanding of the history, principles, and form of government of the United States. There is no exemption from this requirement.

You will also be examined on your ability to read, write, and speak English. If on the date of your examination you are more than 50 years of age and have been a lawful permanent resident for 20 years or more, or you are 55 years of age and have been a lawful permanent resident for at least 15 years, you will be exempt from the English language requirements of the law. If you are exempt, you may take the examination in any language you wish.

Oath of Allegiance. If your application is approved, you will be required to take the following oath of allegiance to the United States in order to become a citizen:

"I hereby declare, on oath, that I absolutely and entirely renounce and abjure all allegiance and fidelity to any foreign prince, potentate, state or sovereignty, of whom or which I have heretofore been a subject or citizen; that I will support and defend the Constitution and laws of the United States of America against all enemies, foreign and domestic; that I will bear true faith and allegiance to the same; that I will bear arms on behalf of the United States when required by the law; that I will perform noncombatant service in the armed forces of the United States when required by the law; that I will perform work of national importance under civilian direction when required by the law; and that I take this obligation freely without any mental reservation or purpose of evasion; so help me God."

If you cannot promise to bear arms or perform noncombatant service because of religious training and belief, you may omit those statements when taking the oath. "Religious training and belief" means a person's belief in relation to a Supreme Being involving duties superior to those arising from any human relation, but does not include essentially political, sociological, or philosophical views or merely a personal moral code.

Oath ceremony. You may choose to have the oath of allegiance administered in a ceremony conducted by the Service or request to be scheduled for an oath ceremony in a court that has jurisdiction over the applicant's place of residence. At the time of your examination you will be asked to elect either form of ceremony. You will become a citizen on the date of the oath ceremony and the Attorney General will issue a Certificate of Naturalization as evidence of United States citizenship.

If you wish to change your name as part of the naturalization process, you will have to take the oath in court.

Penalties.

If you knowingly and willfully falsify or conceal a material fact or submit a false document with this request, we will deny the benefit you are filing for, and may deny any other immigration benefit. In addition, you will face severe penalties provided by law, and may be subject to criminal prosecution.

Privacy Act Notice.

We ask for the information on this form, and associated evidence, to determine if you have established eligibility for the immigration benefit you are filing for. Our legal right to ask for this information is in 8 USC 1439, 1440, 1443, 1445, 1446, and 1452. We may provide this information to other government agencies. Failure to provide this information, and any requested evidence, may delay a final decision or result in denial of your request.

Paperwork Reduction Act Notice.

A person is not required to respond to a collection of information unless it displays a currently valid OMB control number. We try to create forms and instructions that are accurate, can be easily understood, and which impose the least possible burden on you to provide us with information. Often this is difficult because some immigration laws are very complex. Accordingly, the reporting burden for this collection of information is computed as follows: (1) learning about the law and form, 20 minutes; (2) completing the form, 25 minutes; and (3) assembling and filing the application (includes statutory required interview and travel time, after filing of application), 3 hours and 35 minutes, for an estimated average of 4 hours and 20 minutes per response. If you have comments regarding the accuracy of this estimate, or suggestions for making this form simpler, you can write to the Immigration and Naturalization Service, 425 I Street, N.W., Room 5307, Washington, D.C. 20536; OMB No. 1115-0009, **DO NOT MAIL YOUR COMPLETED APPLICATION TO THIS ADDRESS.**

OMB #1115-0009

Application for Naturalization

START HERE - Please Type or Print

Part 1. Information about you.

Family Name	Given Name	Middle Initial

U.S. Mailing Address - Care of

Street Number and Name		Apt. #
City	County	
State	ZIP Code	

Date of Birth (month/day/year)	Country of Birth
Social Security #	A #

Part 2. Basis for Eligibility *(check one).*

a. ☐ I have been a permanent resident for at least five (5) years .

b. ☐ I have been a permanent resident for at least three (3) years and have been married to a United States Citizen for those three years.

c. ☐ I am a permanent resident child of United States citizen parent(s) .

d. ☐ I am applying on the basis of qualifying military service in the Armed Forces of the U.S. and have attached completed Forms N-426 and G-325B

e. ☐ Other. (Please specify section of law)_____ .

Part 3. Additional information about you.

Date you became a permanent resident (month/day/year)	Port admitted with an immmigrant visa or INS Office where granted adjustment of status.
Citizenship	

Name on alien registration card (if different than in Part 1)

Other names used since you became a permanent resident (including maiden name)

Sex	☐ Male ☐ Female	Height		Marital Status:	☐ Single ☐ Married	☐ Divorced ☐ Widowed

Can you speak, read and write English ?   ☐No ☐Yes.

Absences from the U.S.:

Have you been absent from the U.S. since becoming a permanent resident?   ☐ No ☐Yes.

If you answered **"Yes"** , complete the following, Begin with your most recent absence. If you need more room to explain the reason for an absence or to list more trips, continue on separate paper.

Date left U.S.	Date returned	Did absence last 6 months or more?	Destination	Reason for trip
		☐ Yes ☐ No		
		☐ Yes ☐ No		
		☐ Yes ☐ No		
		☐ Yes ☐ No		
		☐ Yes ☐ No		
		☐ Yes ☐ No		

FOR INS USE ONLY

Returned	Receipt
Resubmitted	
Reloc Sent	
Reloc Rec'd	
☐ Applicant Interviewed	

At interview

☐ request naturalization ceremony at court

Remarks

Action

To Be Completed by
Attorney or Representative, if any

☐ Fill in box if G-28 is attached to represent the applicant

VOLAG#

ATTY State License #

Form N-400 (Rev. 01/15/99)N

Part 4. Information about your residences and employment.

A. List your addresses during the last five (5) years or since you became a permanent resident, whichever is less. Begin with your current address. If you need more space, continue on separate paper:

| Street Number and Name, City, State, Country, and Zip Code | Dates (month/day/year) | |
	From	To

B. List your employers during the last five (5) years. List your present or most recent employer first. If none, write "None". If you need more space, continue on separate paper.

| Employer's Name | Employer's Address | | Dates Employed (month/day/year) | | Occupation/position |
	Street Name and Number - City, State and ZIP Code		From	To	

Part 5. Information about your marital history.

A. Total number of times you have been married _____ . If you are now married, complete the following regarding your husband or wife.

Family name	Given name	Middle initial

Address		

Date of birth (month/day/year)	Country of birth	Citizenship
Social Security#	A# (if applicable)	Immigration status (If not a U.S. citizen)

Naturalization (If applicable)
(month/day/year) _____   Place   (City, State)

If you have ever previously been married or if your current spouse has been previously married, please provide the following on separate paper: Name of prior spouse, date of marriage, date marriage ended, how marriage ended and immigration status of prior spouse.

Part 6. Information about your children.

B. Total Number of Children _____ . Complete the following information for each of your children. If the child lives with you, state "with me" in the address column; otherwise give city/state/country of child's current residence. If deceased, write "deceased" in the address column. If you need more space, continue on separate paper.

Full name of child	Date of birth	Country of birth	Citizenship	A - Number	Address

Form N-400 (Rev. 01/15/99) N

Part 7. Additional eligibility factors.

Please answer each of the following questions. If your answer is **"Yes"**, explain on a separate paper.

1. Are you now, or have you ever been a member of, or in any way connected or associated with the Communist Party, or ever knowingly aided or supported the Communist Party directly, or indirectly through another organization, group or person, or ever advocated, taught, believed in, or knowingly supported or furthered the interests of communism? ☐ Yes ☐ No

2. During the period March 23, 1933 to May 8, 1945, did you serve in, or were you in any way affiliated with, either directly or indirectly, any military unit, paramilitary unit, police unit, self-defense unit, vigilante unit, citizen unit of the Nazi party or SS, government agency or office, extermination camp, concentration camp, prisoner of war camp, prison, labor camp, detention camp or transit camp, under the control or affiliated with:
   a. The Nazi Government of Germany? ☐ Yes ☐ No
   b. Any government in any area occupied by, allied with, or established with the assistance or cooperation of, the Nazi Government of Germany? ☐ Yes ☐ No

3. Have you at any time, anywhere, ever ordered, incited, assisted, or otherwise participated in the persecution of any person because of race, religion, national origin, or political opinion? ☐ Yes ☐ No

4. Have you ever left the United States to avoid being drafted into the U.S. Armed Forces? ☐ Yes ☐ No

5. Have you ever failed to comply with Selective Service laws? ☐ Yes ☐ No
   If you have registered under the Selective Service laws, complete the following information:
   Selective Service Number:_____ Date Registered:_____
   If you registered before 1978, also provide the following:
   Local Board Number:_____ Classification:_____

6. Did you ever apply for exemption from military service because of alienage, conscientious objections or other reasons? ☐ Yes ☐ No

7. Have you ever deserted from the military, air or naval forces of the United States? ☐ Yes ☐ No

8. Since becoming a permanent resident, have you ever failed to file a federal income tax return? ☐ Yes ☐ No

9. Since becoming a permanent resident, have you filed a federal income tax return as a nonresident or failed to file a federal return because you considered yourself to be a nonresident? ☐ Yes ☐ No

10 Are deportation proceedings pending against you, or have you ever been deported, or ordered deported, or have you ever applied for suspension of deportation? ☐ Yes ☐ No

11. Have you ever claimed in writing, or in any way, to be a United States citizen? ☐ Yes ☐ No

12. Have you ever:
   a. been a habitual drunkard? ☐ Yes ☐ No
   b. advocated or practiced polygamy? ☐ Yes ☐ No
   c. been a prostitute or procured anyone for prostitution? ☐ Yes ☐ No
   d. knowingly and for gain helped any alien to enter the U.S. illegally? ☐ Yes ☐ No
   e. been an illicit trafficker in narcotic drugs or marijuana? ☐ Yes ☐ No
   f. received income from illegal gambling? ☐ Yes ☐ No
   g. given false testimony for the purpose of obtaining any immigration benefit? ☐ Yes ☐ No

13. Have you ever been declared legally incompetent or have you ever been confined as a patient in a mental institution? ☐ Yes ☐ No

14. Were you born with, or have you acquired in same way, any title or order of nobility in any foreign State? ☐ Yes ☐ No

15. Have you ever:
   a. knowingly committed any crime for which you have not been arrested? ☐ Yes ☐ No
   b. been arrested, cited, charged, indicted, convicted, fined or imprisoned for breaking or violating any law or ordinance excluding traffic regulations? ☐ Yes ☐ No

(If you answer yes to 15 , in your explanation give the following information for each incident or occurrence the **city**, **state**, and **country**, where the offense took place, the **date** and **nature** of the offense, and the **outcome** or **disposition** of the case).

Part 8. Allegiance to the U.S.

If your answer to any of the following questions is **"NO"**, attach a full explanation:
1. Do you believe in the Constitution and form of government of the U.S.? ☐ Yes ☐ No
2. Are you willing to take the full Oath of Allegiance to the U.S.? (see instructions) ☐ Yes ☐ No
3. If the law requires it, are you willing to bear arms on behalf of the U.S.? ☐ Yes ☐ No
4. If the law requires it, are you willing to perform noncombatant services in the Armed Forces of the U.S.? ☐ Yes ☐ No
5. If the law requires it, are you willing to perform work of national importance under civilian direction? ☐ Yes ☐ No

Form N-400 (Rev. 01/15/99)N

Part 9. Memberships and organizations.

A. List your present and past membership in or affiliation with every organization, association, fund, foundation, party, club, society, or similar group in the United States or in any other place. Include any military service in this part. If none, write "none". Include the name of organization, location, dates of membership and the nature of the organization. If additional space is needed, use separate paper.

Part 10. Complete only if you checked block " C " In Part 2.

How many of your parents are U.S. citizens? ☐ One ☐ Both (Give the following about one U.S. citizen parent:)

Family Name	Given Name	Middle Name

Address

Basis for citizenship:
☐ Birth
☐ Naturalization Cert. No.

Relationship to you (check one): ☐ natural parent ☐ adoptive parent
☐ parent of child legitimated after birth

If adopted or legitimated after birth, give date of adoption or, legitimation: *(month/day/year)*_____.

Does this parent have legal custody of you? ☐ Yes ☐ No

(Attach a copy of relating evidence to establish that you are the child of this U.S. citizen and evidence of this parent's citizenship.)

Part 11. Signature. *(Read the information on penalties in the instructions before completing this section).*

I certify or, if outside the United States, I swear or affirm, under penalty of perjury under the laws of the United States of America that this application, and the evidence submitted with it, is all true and correct. I authorize the release of any information from my records which the Immigration and Naturalization Service needs to determine eligibility for the benefit I am seeking.

Signature   Date

Please Note: If you do not completely fill out this form, or fail to submit required documents listed in the instructions, you may not be found eligible for naturalization and this application may be denied.

Part 12. Signature of person preparing form if other than above. *(Sign below)*

I declare that I prepared this application at the request of the above person and it is based on all information of which I have knowledge.

Signature   Print Your Name   Date

Firm Name
and Address

DO NOT COMPLETE THE FOLLOWING UNTIL INSTRUCTED TO DO SO AT THE INTERVIEW

I swear that I know the contents of this application, and supplemental pages 1 through_____, that the corrections , numbered 1 through_____, were made at my request, and that this amended application, is true to the best of my knowledge and belief.

_____
(Complete and true signature of applicant)

Subscribed and sworn to before me by the applicant.

_____
(Examiner's Signature)   Date

Documents you need to include with your N-400:

All applicants must send:
- A photocopy of both sides of your Permanent Resident Card (previously known as Alien Registration Card);
- Two color photographs (¾ frontal image); AND
- A check or money order (for the latest fee see the insert titled "Current Naturalization Fees" in the back pocket of this *Guide*).

If an attorney or accredited representative is acting on your behalf, send:
- Form G-28, "Notice of Entry of Appearance as Attorney or Representative."

If your current name is different than the name on your Permanent Resident Card, send:
- The document which legally changed your name (marriage license, divorce decree, OR court document) OR a detailed explanation of why you use a different name.

If you are applying for naturalization on the basis of marriage to a U.S. citizen, send:
- Proof that your spouse has been a U.S. citizen for at least the past 3 years (birth certificate, naturalization certificate, certificate of citizenship, copy of the inside of the front cover and signature page of your spouse's valid U.S. passport, OR Form FS240, "Report of Birth Abroad of a Citizen of the United States of America");
- Your current marriage certificate;
- Proof of termination of ALL of your spouse's prior marriages (divorce decree OR death certificate); AND
- An original IRS Form 1722 listing tax information for the past 3 years OR copies of the income tax forms you filed for the past 3 years.

If you were previously married, send:
- Proof of termination of ALL of your prior marriages (divorce decree OR death certificate).

If you have ever been in the United States military, send:
- An original Form N-426, "Request for Certification of Military or Naval Service;" AND
- An original Form G-325B, "Biographic Information."

If you have taken a trip outside of the United States that lasted for 6 months or more since becoming a Permanent Resident, send:
- An original IRS Form 1722 listing tax information for the past 5 years (or for the past 3 years if you are applying on the basis of marriage to a U.S. citizen).

If you have a dependent spouse or children and have been ordered to provide financial support, send:
- Copies of the court or government order to provide financial support; AND
- Evidence that you have complied with the court or government order (cancelled checks, money order receipts, a court or agency printout of child support payments, OR evidence of wage garnishments).

If you have ever been arrested or detained by any law enforcement officer for any reason and no charges were filed, send:
- An official statement from the arresting agency or applicable court indicating that no charges were filed.

If you have ever been arrested or detained by any law enforcement officer for any reason and charges were filed, send:
- An original or certified copy of the complete court disposition for each incident (dismissal order, conviction record, OR acquittal order).

If you have ever been convicted or placed in an alternative sentencing program or rehabilitative program, send:
- The sentencing record for each incident; AND
- Evidence that you completed your sentence (probation record, parole record, OR evidence that you completed an alternative sentencing program or rehabilitative program).

If you have ever had any arrest or conviction vacated, set aside, sealed, expunged, or otherwise removed from your record, send:
- An original or certified copy of the court order vacating, setting aside, sealing, expunging, or otherwise removing the arrest or conviction.

If you have ever failed to file an income tax return when it was required by law, send:
- Copies of all correspondence with the Internal Revenue Service (IRS) regarding your failure to file.

If you have any Federal, state, or local taxes that are overdue, send:
- A signed agreement from the IRS, state, or local tax office showing that you have filed a tax return and arranged to pay the taxes you owe; AND
- Documentation from the IRS, state, or local tax office showing the current status of your repayment program.

If you are applying for a disability exception to the testing requirement, send:
- An original Form N-648, "Medical Certification for Disability Exceptions," completed by a licensed medical doctor or licensed clinical psychologist.

If you did not register with the Selective Service and you 1) are male, 2) are 26 years old or older, and 3) lived in the United States in a status other than as a lawful nonimmigrant between the ages of 18 and 26, send:
- •A "Status Information Letter" from the Selective Service (call 1-847-688-6888 for more information).

Citizenship Questions and Answers

To be eligible for naturalization, you have to be able to read, write, and speak basic English. You must also have a basic knowledge of U.S. history and government. The questions on the next five pages are examples of questions an INS officer may ask you at your interview.

Unit 1

U.S. History

1. What country did we fight during the Revolutionary War?

2. What were the 13 original states of the United States called before they were states?

3. What were the 13 original states?

4. Which President was the first Commander in Chief of the U.S. Army and Navy?

5. Who was the first President of the United States?

6. Which President is called the "Father of our Country"?

7. What special group advises the President?

8. Who was the main writer of the Declaration of Independence?

9. What are some of the basic beliefs of the Declaration of Independence?

10. Who said, "Give me liberty or give me death"?

11. When was the Declaration of Independence adopted?

12. In what year was the Constitution written?

13. What is the supreme law of the United States?

14. What is the Constitution?

15. Can the Constitution be changed?

16. What do we call changes to the Constitution?

17. How many changes, or amendments, are there to the Constitution?

18. Whose rights are guaranteed by the Constitution and the Bill of Rights?

19. What is the introduction to the Constitution called?

20. What is the Bill of Rights?

1. England

2. Colonies

3. Virginia, Massachusetts, Maryland, Rhode Island, Connecticut, New Hampshire, North Carolina, South Carolina, New York, New Jersey, Pennsylvania, Delaware, and Georgia

4. George Washington

5. George Washington

6. George Washington

7. The Cabinet

8. Thomas Jefferson

9. That all men are created equal and have the right to life, liberty, and the pursuit of happiness

10. Patrick Henry

11. July 4, 1776

12. 1787

13. The Constitution

14. The supreme law of the land

15. Yes

16. Amendments

17. 27

18. All people living in the United States

19. The Preamble

20. The first ten amendments to the Constitution

21. What are the first 10 amendments to the Constitution called?

21. The Bill of Rights

22. Name one right or freedom guaranteed by the first amendment.

22. The rights of freedom:
    • of speech,
    • of religion,
    • of assembly, and
    • to petition the government

23. Where does freedom of speech come from?

23. The Bill of Rights

24. What is the most important right granted to United States citizens?

24. The right to vote

25. What is the minimum voting age in the United States?

25. 18

26. Name the amendments that guarantee or address voting rights.

26. 15th, 19th, and 26th

27. Name one benefit of being a citizen of the United States.

27. To obtain federal government jobs, to travel with a U.S. passport, or to petition for close relatives to come to the United States to live

28. What Immigration and Naturalization Service form is used to apply for naturalized citizenship?

28. Form N-400 (Application for Naturalization)

29. Who was President during the Civil War?

29. Abraham Lincoln

30. What did the Emancipation Proclamation do?

30. It freed the slaves

31. Name some countries that were our enemies during World War II.

31. Germany, Italy, and Japan

32. Name one purpose of the United Nations.

32. For countries to discuss and try to resolve world problems or to provide economic aid to many countries

Unit 2

U.S. Government

1. How many branches are there in the United States government?

1. 3

2. What are the three branches of our government?

2. Executive, judicial, and legislative

3. What is the legislative branch of our government?

3. Congress

4. What makes up Congress?

4. The Senate and the House of Representatives

5. Who elects Congress?

5. The citizens of the United States

6. How many senators are there in Congress?

6. 100

7. Why are there 100 senators in the United States Senate?

7. Each state elects two

8. How many voting members are there in the House of Representatives?

8. 435

9. Who makes the federal laws in the United States?	9. Congress
10. What group has the power to declare war?	10. Congress
11. Who meets in the U.S. Capitol building?	11. Congress
12. What is the United States Capitol?	12. The place where Congress meets
13. For how long do we elect each senator?	13. 6 years
14. For how long do we elect each member of the House of Representatives?	14. 2 years
15. How many times may a senator or congressman be re-elected?	15. No limit
16. What is the executive branch of our government?	16. The President, the Cabinet, and departments under the Cabinet members
17. Who is the head of the executive branch of the U.S. government?	17. The President
18. Who elects the President of the United States?	18. The electoral college
19. What is the White House?	19. The President's official home
20. What is the name of the President's official home?	20. The White House
21. Where is the White House located?	21. Washington, D.C.
22. Who signs bills into law?	22. The President
23. Who is the Commander in Chief of the United States military?	23. The President
24. Who becomes our President if the President dies?	24. The Vice President
25. Who becomes President if both the President and Vice President die?	25. Speaker of the House
26. For how long is the President elected?	26. 4 years
27. In what month do we vote for the President?	27. November
28. In what month is the new President inaugurated?	28. January
29. How many full terms can a President serve?	29. 2
30. What are some of the requirements to be eligible to become President?	30. Candidates for President must: • be natural born citizens, • be at least 35 years old, • have lived in the United States for at least 14 years
31. Who is the President of the United States today?	31. George W. Bush
32. Who is the Vice President of the United States today?	32. Dick Cheney

33. Name the highest part of the judiciary branch of our government.

33. The Supreme Court

34. What are the duties of the Supreme Court?

34. To interpret and explain the law

35. What is the highest court in the United States?

35. The Supreme Court

36. Who nominates judges for the Supreme Court?

36. The President

37. How many Supreme Court justices are there?

37. 9

38. Who is the Chief Justice of the Supreme Court?

38. William Rehnquist

39. What was the 49th state added to our Union (the United States)?

39. Alaska

40. What was the 50th state added to our Union (the United States)?

40. Hawaii

41. How many states are there in the Union (the United States)?

41. 50

42. What is the capital of the state you live in?

42. _____

43. Name the two senators from your state.

43. _____

_____

44. What is the head executive of a state government called?

44. Governor

45. Who is the current governor of the state you live in?

45. _____

46. What is the head executive of a city government called?

46. Mayor

47. What kind of government does the United States have?

47. A republic

48. What are the two major political parties in the United States today?

48. Democratic and Republican

Unit 3

U.S. Celebrations

1. What holiday was celebrated for the first time by the American colonists?

1. Thanksgiving

2. Why did the Pilgrims come to America?

2. To gain religious freedom

3. What is the name of the ship that brought the Pilgrims to America?

3. The *Mayflower*

4. Who helped the Pilgrims in America?

4. Native Americans/American Indians

5. What do we celebrate on the Fourth of July?

5. Independence Day

6. Independence Day celebrates independence from whom?

6. England

7. Who wrote the "Star-Spangled Banner"?

7. Francis Scott Key

8. What is the national anthem of the United States?	**8.** The "Star-Spangled Banner"
9. What are the colors of our flag?	**9.** Red, white, and blue
10. What color are the stars on our flag?	**10.** White
11. What color are the stripes on the flag?	**11.** Red and white
12. How many stars are there on our flag?	**12.** 50
13. How many stripes are there on the flag?	**13.** 13
14. What do the stars on the flag mean?	**14.** One for each state
15. What do the stripes on the flag represent?	**15.** The first 13 states
16. Who was Martin Luther King, Jr.?	**16.** A civil rights leader

Sentences for Dictation and Reading

The sentences on the next two pages are examples of the types of sentences an INS officer may ask you to read aloud or write during your interview.

Civics History

Citizens have the right to vote.

_____

Congress passes laws in the United States.

_____

George Washington was the first President.

_____

I want to be an American citizen.

_____

Many people come to America for freedom.

_____

Our government is divided into three branches.

_____

People vote for the President in November.

_____

The Constitution is the supreme law of our land.

_____

The House and Senate are parts of Congress.

_____

The President is elected every 4 years.

_____

The President signs bills into law.

_____

The White House is in Washington, D.C.

_____

The United States flag is red, white, and blue.

_____

There are 50 states in the Union.

_____

Everyday Life

He came to live with his brother.

_____

He wanted to find a job.

_____

She can speak English very well.

_____

The teacher was proud of her class.

_____

They buy many things at the store.

_____

She was happy with her house.

_____

I came here for my interview.

_____

We are very smart to learn this.

_____

The boy threw a ball.

_____

I drive a blue car to work.

_____

Today is a sunny day.

_____

The children play at school.

_____

They are a very happy family.

_____

It is a good job to start with.

_____

Questions and Answers for the 65/20 Exception

If you are over 65 and have lived in the United States for at least 20 years, an INS officer may ask you these questions in your language.

1. Why do we celebrate the Fourth of July?
2. Who was the first President of the United States?
3. Who is the President of the United States now?
4. What is the Constitution?
5. What are the first 10 amendments to the Constitution called?
6. Who elects Congress?
7. How many senators are there in Congress?
8. For how long do we elect each senator?
9. For how long do we elect each member of the House of Representatives?
10. Who nominates judges to the Supreme Court?
11. What are the three branches of our government?
12. What is the highest court in the United States?
13. What major river running north to south divides the United States?
14. The Civil War was fought over what important issues?
15. What are the two major political parties in the United States today?
16. How many states are there in the United States?
17. What is the capital of the United States?
18. What is the minimum voting age in the United States?
19. Who was Martin Luther King, Jr.?
20. What nation was first to land a man on the moon?
21. What is the capital of your state?
22. What is it called if the President refuses to sign a bill into law and returns it to Congress with his objections?
23. What two oceans border the United States?
24. What famous American invented the electric light bulb?
25. What is the national anthem of the United States?

1. It is Independence Day
2. George Washington
3. George W. Bush
4. The supreme law of the land
5. The Bill of Rights
6. The citizens of the United States
7. 100
8. 6 years
9. 2 years
10. The President
11. Legislative, executive, and judicial
12. The Supreme Court
13. The Mississippi River
14. Slavery and state's rights
15. Democratic and Republican
16. 50
17. Washington, D.C.
18. 18
19. A civil rights leader
20. The United States
21. _____
22. Veto
23. The Atlantic and Pacific Oceans
24. Thomas Edison
25. The "Star-Spangled Banner"

92

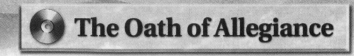

The Oath of Allegiance

After you pass the citizenship test, you say the Oath of Allegiance and become a U.S. citizen.

I hereby declare, on oath;

that I absolutely and entirely renounce and abjure

all allegiance and fidelity to any foreign prince,

potentate, state, or sovereignty, of whom or which

I have heretofore been a subject or citizen;

that I will support and defend the Constitution and the

laws of the United States of America against all enemies,

foreign and domestic;

that I will bear true faith and allegiance to the same;

that I will bear arms on behalf of the United States when

required by the law;

that I will perform noncombatant service in the Armed

Forces of the United States when required by the law;

that I will perform work of national importance under

civilian direction when required by the law; and

that I take this obligation freely, without any mental

reservation or purpose of evasion; so help me God.

Answer Key

Unit 1, U.S. History

⭐ Lesson 1   Page 11

Complete the dialogs.

Revolutionary War, colonies, George Washington, President, Father Independence, England, Declaration, Thomas Jefferson, equal

⭐ Lesson 2   Page 16

Complete the puzzle.

Across: **1.** Preamble   **5.** Constitution   **6.** speech   **7.** vote

Down: **2.** amendment   **3.** Rights   **4.** citizen

⭐ Lesson 3   Page 20

Complete the sentences.

1. slavery   **2.** Abraham Lincoln   **3.** Confederate   **4.** Emancipation Proclamation   **5.** Union

Complete the puzzle.

Across: **2.** Emancipation   **5.** united

Down: **1.** divided   **3.** Civil   **4.** Lee   **5.** Union

⭐ Lesson 4   Page 24

Circle *true* or *false*.

1. true   **2.** false   **3.** false   **4.** true   **5.** false   **6.** false   **7.** true   **8.** true

Rewrite the false sentences to make them true.

1. The United States fought against Germany and Austria-Hungary in World War I. OR: The United States fought with Russia in World War I.   **2.** The Great Depression happened before World War II. OR: The Great Depression happened after World War I.   **3.** The United States entered World War II in 1941.   **4.** The United States fought against Germany, Italy, and Japan in World War II. OR: The United States fought with France in World War II.

⭐ Lesson 5   Page 27

Match.

1. c. 1954   **2. g.** South Vietnam   **3. e.** North Vietnam   **4. d.** John F. Kennedy   **5. h.** 1963   **6. b.** Lyndon Johnson   **7. a.** protested   **8. f.** 1973

U.S. History Checkup   Pages 28–31

1. 1776   **2.** Freedom of speech   **3.** Form N-400, Application for Naturalization   **4.** Abraham Lincoln   **5.** George Washington   **6.** The supreme law of the land   **7.** George Washington   **8.** All people living in the United States   **9.** An amendment   **10.** George Washington   **11.** Virginia, Massachusetts, Maryland, Rhode Island, Connecticut, New Hampshire, North Carolina, South Carolina, New York, New Jersey, Pennsylvania, Delaware, Georgia   **12.** Abraham Lincoln   **13.** The right to vote   **14.** The Preamble   **15.** The first 10 amendments to the Constitution   **16.** Germany   **17.** That all men are created equal   **18.** The Bill of Rights   **19.** 27   **20.** England   **21.** To discuss and try to resolve world problems   **22.** George Washington   **23.** The Bill of Rights   **24.** 1787   **25.** The Cabinet   **26.** 18   **27.** It freed the slaves   **28.** Colonies   **29.** Patrick Henry   **30.** Thomas Jefferson   **31.** The Constitution   **32.** Germany, Italy, and Japan

Unit 2, U.S. Government

⭐ **Lesson 6**   **Page 37**

Complete the chart.

The House of Representatives
1. 435
2. 2
4. 25

The Senate
1. 2, 100
2. 6
4. 30

⭐ **Lesson 7**   **Page 41**

Complete the chart.
1. The Vice President   2. The President
3. The President   4. The Vice President
5. The President

Complete the sentences.
1. 4   2. 2   3. 35   4. 14   5. November
6. January   7. George W. Bush   8. Dick Cheney

⭐ **Lesson 8**   **Page 45**

Complete the sentences.
1. Supreme Court   2. Chief Justice
3. President   4. Congress

Complete the chart.
1. Executive   2. Legislative   3. Judicial

⭐ **Lesson 9**   **Page 47**

Complete the sentences
Check your answers with your instructor.

Circle your state and state capital.   **Page 48**
Check your map with your instructor.

Plan a trip.   **Page 49**
1. Massachusetts—Boston   2. New York—Albany   3. Ohio—Columbus   4. Illinois—Springfield   5. Florida—Tallahassee
6. Louisiana—Baton Rouge   7. Texas—Austin   8. New Mexico—Santa Fe
9. Arizona—Phoenix   10. California—Sacramento

⭐ **Lesson 10**   **Page 52**

Complete the chart.
Check your chart with your instructor.

Complete the chart.   **Page 53**
1. State Government   2. Local Government
3. Federal Government   4. Federal Government, State Government
5. Local Government

Complete the sentences.
1. republic   2. two   3. Republican
4. branches

U.S. Government Checkup   **Pages 54–57**
1. William Rehnquist   2. The Supreme Court
3. Executive, Judicial, Legislative   4. Where Congress meets   5. To interpret and explain laws   6. Each state elects 2   7. The citizens of the United States   8. November   9. 3
10. Alaska and Hawaii   11. The White House   12. In Washington, D.C., at 1600 Pennsylvania Avenue   13. The Speaker of the House of Representatives   14. The President   15. Congress   16. 9   17. George W. Bush   18. Must have served as a governor   19. The President, the Cabinet, and the departments under the Cabinet
20. Democratic and Republican   21. The President   22. The President   23. 100
24. The Senate and the House of Representatives   25. Congress   26. January
27. The electoral college   28. Congress
29. 4 years   30. The Vice President
31. Governor   32. 2

Unit 3, U.S. Celebrations

★ **Lesson 11**   **Page 62**

Complete the puzzle.

Across: **2.** Native Americans **4.** Pilgrims
  5. freedom
Down: **1.** meal **2.** November **3.** Mayflower

★ **Lesson 12**   **Page 67**

Complete the puzzle.

Across: **5.** Declaration **6.** parade
Down: **1.** stripe **2.** July **3.** Banner
  4. Union

Complete the sentences.

  1. stripe **2.** Union **3.** Banner **4.** July
  5. parade **6.** Declaration

★ **Lesson 13**   **Page 71**

Circle the dates of these holidays.

  1. Martin Luther King, Jr. Day—January 21
  2. Presidents' Day—February 18

  3. Memorial Day—May 27
  4. Flag Day—June 14
  5. Independence Day—July 4
  6. Labor Day—September 2

U.S. Celebrations Checkup   **Pages 72–73**

1. 13 **2.** The *Mayflower* **3.** 50 **4.** Native Americans/American Indians **5.** A civil rights leader **6.** The "Star-Spangled Banner" **7.** Red and white **8.** The first 13 states **9.** To gain religious freedom **10.** 50 **11.** England **12.** One for each state **13.** Francis Scott Key **14.** Independence Day **15.** Thanksgiving **16.** July 4